TAKE THE LEAD

Interpersonal skills for project managers

DAVID BODDY

University of Glasgow Business School

DAVID BUCHANAN

Loughborough University Business School

PRENTICE HALL

New York   London   Toronto   Tokyo   Sydney   Singapore

First published 1992 by
Prentice Hall International (UK) Ltd
Campus 400, Maylands Avenue
Hemel Hempstead
Hertfordshire, HP2 7EZ
A division of
Simon & Schuster International Group

Typeset in 10/12 pt Times
by Columns Design & Production Services Ltd, Reading

Printed and bound in Great Britain by
Hartnolls, Bodmin, Cornwall

Library of Congress Cataloging-in-Publication Data

Boddy, David.
  Take the lead : interpersonal skills for project managers / David Boddy and David A.
  Buchanan.
  p. cm.
  Includes bibliographical references and index.
  ISBN 0–13–812827–8 (pbk)
  1. Industrial project management.   2. Organizational change—Management.
  I. Buchanan, David A.   II. Title.
  HD69.P75B63   1992   92–3946
  658.4'04—dc20   CIP

British Library Cataloguing in Publication Data

A catalogue record for this book is available from the British Library
ISBN 0–13–812827–8 (pbk)

---

1 2 3 4 5   96 95 94 93 92

Contents

Preface

The manager who is able and willing to achieve significant change in the organization has a bright future. The business environment is turbulent, and organizations are having to change what they do, and how they do it, much more rapidly than was once the case. Someone has to be responsible for putting these changes into effect, for managing the practical detail, for making the change happen.

This book is for such people. It will show them how to take the lead in change, how to manage it confidently and effectively. They can do this by using quite basic management skills and practices, which are not hard to acquire – yet which make the management of major change projects satisfying and rewarding.

Acknowledgements

This book was made possible by the cooperation and support of many people. Peter Reid, and later David Vickers, at the Training Agency provided support and encouragement throughout the project. Mike Buckingham and Des Barrett kindly agreed to join a project steering group, enabling us to test our ideas and preliminary conclusions against their vast practical experience.

We also received help from many other managers who gave us the benefit of their experience in managing change projects; it is upon this experience that the book is based, and without their help it could not exist.

Nan Gray organized the research phase of the project, and Maureen Christie prepared the material for publication; our grateful thanks to them both for working, as usual, to the highest standards.

David Boddy and David Buchanan

For Cynthia

PART I
The setting

1

The job of managing change

How this book will help you manage change

This book is designed to give practical guidance to those who are responsible for planning and managing changes within organizations. In turbulent times, there is a lot of change to be managed – and someone has to turn the bright idea into the practical reality. It will show what the job involves, and how, by the use of quite basic skills and practices, awkward changes can be made manageable.

The title of such people will vary. Sometimes the task will be done largely by the line manager of the area concerned, alongside his or her normal duties. In other cases, the work will be done by people from a support function – management services, information technology, planning or personnel – working alongside the line manager. These people have such titles as project manager, project planner, internal consultant, business analyst. The titles do not matter – the common characteristic of all such managers is that they are expected to deliver a major change into a working organization on time, and within budget.

The book is intended to give practical guidance to those doing this type of job:

- It will provide a map of the stages and activities in managing change, and where the project manager fits in.
- It will show how others have handled these activities.
- It will identify key features in change projects.
- It will present the three agendas that need to be managed.
- It will identify the interpersonal skills that give the manager a lead in change.
- It will give personal checkpoints for the manager.

The book proposes a new emphasis in the management of change projects. The volatile and competitive business environment means that many change projects are highly uncertain activities. Conventional structured methods of project management are of limited value in novel, ambiguous changes. To reduce the uncertainty in such situations, to turn an ambiguous task into something more definable, requires a different approach. It calls for more attention to be given to the processes and politics of change, and the use of a range of interpersonal skills.

These skills are not new or unusual, and are relatively easy to acquire. By building this part of their repertoire, project managers will be able to make incremental, and sustainable improvements in the way they do the job.

In this chapter we set the scene, dealing with the following:

What kinds of change?
Managing systems and managing change.
What is different about managing change?
Unusual features of the book.

What kinds of change?

Most managers can very quickly identify many changes that are taking place in their organization, or which are being actively considered. Although the changes are different, experience shows that the management problems to be solved will be similar. So the management activities outlined in this book are likely to be needed in any major change. Here is a list of changes which were being managed by one group of managers with whom we recently worked:

- Culture-change in a local authority service.
- New facility in an oil-refining company.
- European-wide order-processing system in a computer company.
- Computer-aided draughting system in an engineering company.
- Payment system change in a local authority.
- Computerized maintenance system in a utility business.
- New product development in an electronics manufacturer.
- Technical innovation in a surveying business.

Each seems unique – and, in many ways, is. But the descriptions illustrate four themes or elements which, in varying proportions, are present in all change situations. These elements are as follows:

1. Task
   (a) developing a new product or service;
   (b) changing the overall direction or mission of the enterprise;
   (c) changing the emphasis given to a particular market;
   (d) new focus in parts of the business (e.g. quality improvement).
2. Structure
   (a) rearranging department functions and responsibilities;
   (b) changing communication and coordination channels;
   (c) changing culture and management style;
   (d) centralizing or decentralizing responsibilities and tasks;
   (e) introducing new job evaluation or payment systems;
   (f) altering relations with other organizations.

The elements of change in a service organization

A newly appointed director of a public service organization which had experienced severe recruitment and retention problems, and which was not providing an acceptable level of service, set out to improve and redefine the service (**Task**). He centralized some functions, changed the roles of junior managers so that they spent less time on administration, and more with customers, and introduced new communications procedures between units, and between the units and the centre (**Structure**). To achieve the centralization there had to be changes in building structure and location, and investment in computer facilities (**Technology**). It was also decided to change the work of junior staff, and to back this up with changes in recruitment practice and training systems (**People**).

The elements of change in a steel business

As the market for steel became more competitive, a Dutch steel company decided it was necessary to focus efforts more consciously on the needs of particular groups of customer (**Task**). Changes in divisional responsibilities were made, from a functional, production-centred form, to a product-centred form. Each new group would concentrate on certain types of demand (**Structure**). This in turn meant that one very large piece of equipment was now in the wrong place, physically separate from the division which made most use of it.

A project manager was briefed to move the equipment from one location on the site, to another about five kilometres away. Preparing the new position, dismantling the machinery, transporting it and re-erecting it would inevitably mean some loss of production; for market reasons that period had to be kept as brief as possible. A great deal of difficult engineering work had to be done (**Technology**), which was backed up by measures to ensure that the skills needed to operate the plant were also transferred (**People**).

3. Technology
    (a) changes in physical plant and equipment;
    (b) introducing new or enhanced computer systems;
    (c) changes in plant or office location or layout;
    (d) creating new facilities on an existing site;
    (e) new communications media.
4. People
    (a) changes in working arrangements of individuals and groups;
    (b) programmes to enhance skills and performance;
    (c) attitude change (e.g. customer care programmes);
    (d) team-working.

In some change projects one element is clearly dominant, with little attention given to, or required by, the others. More usually, successful change management requires attention to all four elements, as most large change projects contain all of them to some degree.

A change which seems at first sight to be mainly a matter of organization may in practice require attention to technical matters. Or one that appears to be mainly technical may in reality have substantial organizational or people elements. Changes set off ripples. When these meet the other elements, the results are sometimes predictable; at other times they take the project manager by surprise.

The four elements can also be thought of as levers for change, or as points of entry to the change process. The links between them mean that the objective of a change project can be approached indirectly. For example, if the change is intended to alter the way people in the organization work, the manager may decide to make some structural changes, in the hope that this will indirectly encourage the change being sought.

As we shall see, effective project management means looking beyond the most visible features of a change. It means seeing the other dimensions, and being able to handle the job as a whole.

So most change projects have, in varying degrees, these common elements – the effective manager recognizes this, and leads the project accordingly. The other common element of change is that the project manager needs to deploy a range of process skills, especially to deal with the organizational, human and political issues which will arise.

Managing systems and managing change

We need to be clear about the differences between managing change projects, and managing in general – and to ask whether they are always different. The task of managing a system, whether a production or a service operation, is conventionally seen as one of managing stability – getting things done by employees and procedures within relatively stable working relationships, using information from reasonably regular and constant sources. From time to time, of course, a change occurs, as a new product, or a new working arrangement is introduced. That is seen as an exceptional, often incremental, disturbance, after which the intention is to return the system to its normal, predictable routines.

> 'Some tasks are ongoing, routine affairs; while others are projects, associated with some kind of change.'

In contrast, projects are conventionally seen as something separate and distinct from the normal activities of the organization. They mean managing change, requiring separate systems and unusual management structures. Often this is the case; projects to create a new physical facility, to create a new market in a different part of the world, to develop a new product in the research lab – these are clearly not part of the regular operation.

Is managing a project different from managing a system? Some ideas are given in Table 1.1. The left-hand column indicates the management processes undertaken in an established system; that on the right indicates those typical of a project.

Table 1.1 Managing systems and managing change

	System	*Project*
Task	Familiar	Unfamiliar
Staff	Designated, known	Diverse, temporary
Roles and duties	Established patterns	Uncertain, variable
Culture	Role or power	Task
Working relationships	Established cooperation	Negotiable
Authority	Clear, reflects position	Ambiguous, little direct
Coordination	Hierarchical	Network/matrix
Information sources	Established, routine	New, uncertain
Learning and attitude change	Desirable	Essential
Momentum	Maintained by system	Threatened by system
Time horizon	Extended, long-term	Bounded, finite

These differences are becoming less clear-cut. Several surveys have confirmed what many managers have personally experienced: that organizations of all kinds are facing much more competitive and changeable conditions than they previously had to cope with. Organizations are therefore having to become more responsive and adaptable to market needs and competitive moves, to change the way they are structured (and to do so more frequently) and to expect more flexible and creative patterns of behaviour from their staff

All of this affects the jobs of managers. As product life cycles shorten, and as technology provides new ways of producing goods and services, exceptional disturbances are no longer, in many types of business, 'one-off' events, but a regular part of the line manager's job. Changes are introduced into the working system which have deadlines, requirements, budgets and ambiguity; and which need the coordination of individuals and resources to adapt the operation to the new circumstances. The line manager's job then is to manage a series of projects. A critical aspect of the job is to get the current product running smoothly, so that the manager can concentrate on reshaping the system for the next new product, or the next change in method.

Managing by project

A recent article in *Management Today* (Jan. 1991, p. 84) showed how some businesses are being reorganized around projects, breaking what were routine activities into separate projects. It gave as an example BREL, an engineering company, which now manages its activities entirely as projects, so that staff from different functions can act together to achieve defined goals, and react quickly in the light of unforeseen problems. This is assisted by a flatter management hierarchy, and the availability of modern information systems.

If businesses are being so organized, many of the techniques and skills we discuss here will apply to those who are managing 'routine' operations. They will be dealing with many of the issues normally associated with more visible 'change' projects.

Another point to be clear about is the term 'project management'. This came into widespread use in the construction industry, and carries with it a sense of tangible, physical results. It implies something with a clear objective or goal, and a fixed time-scale; an identifiable beginning and an identifiable end – at which point the job can be described as complete. It also implies a unique, non-routine activity of limited duration, which draws as required on the coordinated skills and experience of a variety of people, as required.

Project managers face the triple constraints of time, money and the specification. Effective use of people with diverse skills, who because of the uniqueness of the project are constantly forming new relationships, makes the task difficult to control. It is hard to gather and collate information about the state of the job. To overcome those problems of uncertainty, many techniques have been created to move the project through a relatively predictable set of steps or phases. They use structured methods to plan and control activities, so as to keep the whole job on target.

Many projects fit that description, but those we are concerned with in this book do not. In one sense they are similar, in that they involve bringing together people with different skills and outlooks. But they are different in that the changes we consider here typically involve much ambiguity about what the end result will look like, how widely that result will be accepted, and about how to get there. One manager with whom we worked expressed it well:

> The change is not a project as such, with a predefined start and end, but rather it is a programme of continuous change.

This uncertainty or lack of structure is not due to any inability on the part of management; it is inherent in the nature of the changes being introduced, and the uncertain environment in which the work will be done. This makes it much less likely that all the problems can be handled by the use of a structured project management methodology, and much more likely that the emphasis needs to move towards the human, organizational and political aspects of the change.

So terms such as 'project management' are misleading, by implying that we offer a structured method, which clearly we do not. Common phrases which better describe the sense of the book are 'change management', 'managing change' or variations of these. These, however, can sound vague, and are not commonly used by those who do this kind of work. We shall therefore use the terms 'project management', 'change management' and their derivatives interchangeably – to describe changes that are relatively unstructured, with unclear starting points, which cannot usually call on established or structured methods to achieve the result, and where the end-point will be open to different views and interpretations.

What is different about managing change?

Novelty

Implementing a change in an organization is bound to be unique, as it will not have been done in exactly the same way before. The degree of novelty will vary, and may be trivial. Where the novelty factor is high, there will be much uncertainty about what the change can achieve, and how best to get there. This can readily lead to conflicts, errors and omissions in planning and implementing the change.

Unpredictability

It is easy to underestimate how time-consuming a change will be. This can deprive the project and its manager of the time and resources they need to do the job, leading to corners being cut, with the consequent danger of failure and recrimination all round.

Ripples

Changes in one area frequently set off ripples elsewhere. These need to be managed if they are not to disrupt the change. Project managers have to influence people or events over which they have no direct authority; and this task becomes especially difficult if the project is raising issues of policy in other areas, over which there are differences of view.

Clusters

Change is more frequent, and comes in clusters. Almost all the projects with which we have worked have taken place at the same time as other major changes were being undertaken. Sometimes these were other aspects of the same broad project,

---

Multiple change at a bank

A bank undertook a project to introduce a new job evaluation scheme for all its staff, after a long period in which few organizational innovations had occurred. The analysis was long and complex; it was made more so by the facts that during the project the bank was taken over by an overseas bank, and that at the same time the computer system used for personnel matters was being replaced, thus delaying many of the analyses needed for the job evaluation project.

---

and therefore were to be expected. More often the turbulent environment of the organization was prompting several simultaneous responses.

Multi-project situations bring more uncertainty. There will be more competition for resources, and more scepticism as staff observe yet another change being launched.

Rising expectations

There is often a business pressure to get things up and working, and a staff pressure to be consulted. The world has, for many organizations, become tougher, more competitive and perhaps less predictable. Senior managers, or parent organizations, subject to these pressures, pass them down the line. They expect the results quickly, and become impatient with delays and excuses. They may also not fully appreciate the problems facing those planning and implementing the change, leading to pressure for short cuts, with all the dangers that implies.

Conflicting pressures

'Get the system $\rightarrow$ Project $\leftarrow$ 'Make sure the staff
working' manager are consulted'

At the same time, educated and knowledgeable staff, or simply staff who want to express an opinion, are increasingly likely to expect full and careful consultation – especially if the change involves modification to established attitudes, beliefs or values. On a major project, perhaps involving staff at distant locations, this may appear as a source of delay; and thus as a source of conflict with the expectations for speedy results.

These pressures need not be in conflict. As we shall see, effective use of interpersonal skills will enable the manager to meet both sets of expectations simultaneously.

Unusual features of this book

There are many good books about managing projects, usually dealing with the structured aspects of the task, where well-established techniques of analysis, planning and control can be applied. They are typically directed at construction projects or large computer projects, in which external factors affect the project in relatively predictable ways, so that they can be planned for. They also concentrate on projects that are 'free-standing' creations, rather than changes that are embedded in the operations of the enterprise.

This book is different. It deals with organizational and other changes which are novel, and where there are usually different interests at stake. Not only is the outside world likely to be changing during these projects; so too will the attitudes and actions of the interested parties. That implies that political and interpersonal aspects of change will matter; and the book gives much attention to these.

It also recognizes the reality of managing difficult and often controversial projects, and does not seek to present an idealized view of the process. It identifies the obstacles that get in the way of applying good practice, and helps the manager to discover ways of overcoming these. And if the preferred methods do not work, what other lines of action might be available? There is often a difference between the way managers dealing with change would like to act, and the way they are obliged to act to get the job done within the time and resources available.

Above all, the book is based on the recent, actual experience of project managers. The core of that experience was provided by a group of eight managers, each of whom was responsible for introducing a major change into their department or organization. They provided us with an audio-taped 'diary' of their reflections on a recent or current change programme for which they were responsible. They were asked, in an introductory brief, to dictate on tape, in their own time, a narrative account of their job that described the change programme, the context in which it took place, and the expected and actual results.

They were also asked to recall critical incidents in the change programme, how they arose and how they were handled, with an assessment of how well they were handled. The tapes were then transcribed, and given to their producers for additions and amendments. We then had eight first-hand accounts, by the people who were doing the job, of what it felt like to be handling a major change – the difficulties, stresses, conflicts, misunderstandings, and, of course, the solutions and successes.

This activity was seen as a valued exercise by the managers who took part. They welcomed the chance to reflect on the work they had been doing, and also to talk about those experiences, the contrasts and the similarities, with other managers who had been through an equally challenging change management experience.

This novel method was a credible research tool. It provided many new insights into the working lives of contemporary project managers, and what they needed to be able to do to function effectively. To our knowledge, these issues have not previously been studied in such a direct way.

We then conducted a wider questionnaire survey, published in the April 1989 edition of the journal *Management Services*. This was intended to test the wider applicability of the findings from the small sample of managers who had kept an audio-diary. Readers of the journal, with experience of managing change, were asked to comment on that experience in a relatively structured way, and to return the questionnaire to us for analysis.

The results and implications from the diary exercise, and from the questionnaire survey, were then presented to three focus groups, attended in all by some forty managers. These groups provided an opportunity to expose the results to the target audience. It allowed us to check our interpretation of the data, to discuss whether it matched the experience of those at the focus groups, and to clarify the implications for those managing change of the messages coming through.

The work, and the conclusions we were drawing from it, were reported to quarterly meetings of the Steering Group which we had established for the project. This consisted of representatives from the Training Agency who had sponsored the research, ourselves and two senior industrial managers with wide experience of managing major projects.

In addition, our teaching brings us into regular contact with many managers deeply engaged in the processes we are describing. Many of the ideas from the study have been introduced into our management courses, and many of those attending have chosen to prepare assignments and project reports on the topic, usually based on changes which they were themselves undertaking. This has provided a further source of ideas, and a further means of testing the validity and realism of the account.

We have tried to present our views about the job of managing change in as readable a form as possible. The book is intended to be read by people who are busy with a change project – and who therefore want us to get to the point. It aims to provide a road map for those managing change, thus helping to avoid some of the hazards and pitfalls. Something always goes wrong in major changes – the book may help to reduce the unanticipated problems hitting the project manager.

Each chapter contains the following:

- An outline of useful ideas about the topic of the chapter.
- Illustrations and examples from real projects.
- Activities and techniques derived from the text which project managers can use to manage their own projects.
- 'Notepads' containing questions or checklists to help managers review their change projects, in relation to the ideas put forward.
- Personal checkpoints.

The book is organized around this map of the change process, shown in Fig. 1.1. It has three parts. The first looks at the setting in which the project takes place, and within which it has to be managed. The second concentrates on the skills which the manager needs to use to make change happen, while the third presents some ideas about the wider aspects of the change process.

Real projects are usually messy, complicated affairs. The manager grappling with that awkward reality is right to be sceptical of neatly packaged solutions. Although for ease of explanation we use the map in Fig. 1.1, we are well aware that reality is not as simple, and we recognize this reality in the text.

Notepad

- *Write a brief account of the project you are managing.*
- *Which of the elements in 'What kinds of change?' are present?*
- *How do they affect each other?*
- *How might you use change in one area to 'lever' change in another?*

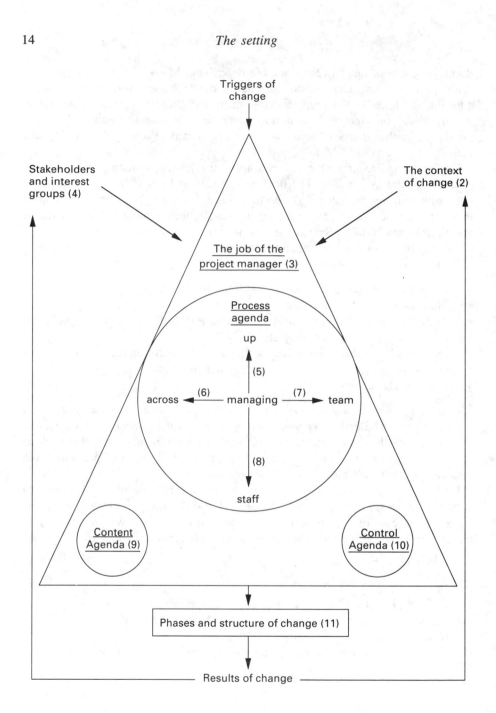

Note: The relevant chapters for each element are indicated in brackets.

Figure 1.1 The job of managing change

2

Each project is different

What are the key features?

A manager responsible for achieving change needs to sense what the job will be like, where the pitfalls will be and which matters will need attention. This chapter provides some guidelines on what to look for.

Each project is unique, in that nobody will have made that change, in that organization, in those circumstances. The degree of uniqueness varies. A programme to change radically the layout of a large purpose-built manufacturing facility will only happen once; introducing a new company procedure into the seventy-fifth branch of a retail chain is not likely to be so different from the previous seventy-four. But it will look unique to the people in the branch, so it is wise to expect differences, and to be alert to the variety of circumstances surrounding a change. The effective project leader acknowledges diversity and seeks to use it, rather than to suppress it.

Uniqueness does not mean there are no guidelines. Projects have identifiable features, which imply different approaches. The project manager who is aware of the landscape being crossed knows what to expect, and what that may mean for the job. The themes of this chapter are as follows:

What forces are driving or restraining the change?
What kind of change is it?
What is the context of the change?
Where are the pitfalls?

What forces are driving or restraining the change?

The flow of information and events within and around an organization contains countless signals about the state of the enterprise, and about external events relevant to its health. Some pass by without impact or response; others arouse a flicker of interest, a burst of activity, perhaps even a feasibility study – and then fade; others set in motion work that leads to significant change.

When such signals have set in motion a change programme which has become the responsibility of a project manager or team, the flow does not cease. Information and events continue to swirl around the project, sometimes helping it along, sometimes disrupting it. They may set off change elsewhere, which affects projects already in progress.

A practical way of using this information is to distinguish between those forces that are driving the change, and those that are restraining it. Driving forces are those that encourage change from the present position. They encourage people and groups to give up past practice, and to act in ways that support the change. Restraining forces are those that induce opposition to the change, or encourage inertia and the maintenance of existing practice.

In order to get movement from the present situation, the driving forces need to be greater than the restraining ones. Project managers can encourage movement by reinforcing and stressing the driving forces – stressing the advantages of the change, making the benefits more attractive. Alternatively they can seek to reduce or diminish the restraining forces, by showing that the problems are not as great as feared, that the difficulties will be temporary.

Experience suggests that it is easier to get movement by reducing the restraining forces. If effort is put into increasing the driving forces, the resisting forces are likely to increase correspondingly, as defensive positions are strengthened.

External events can trigger and drive change: competition, legislation, technical developments, environmental factors, the activities of a pressure group, a presentation by a consultant, visits to an exhibition, a chance conversation – information from any of these sources can trigger a change, and, if used by powerful people, become a driving force for change.

An external driving force

A company manufacturing and distributing bitumen for use on roads supplied a significant part of the market by delivering the material in drums. The empty drums were either disposed of by the contractor, or returned to the company for cleaning and reuse. The waste bitumen which this produced was seen to be an environmental hazard. The management of the company set up a project to reduce or eliminate the sale of bitumen in drums. This was achieved by developing a new piece of road-laying equipment, and by associated changes in the distribution system.

External factors provide a source of justification, a way of legitimizing large-scale change. Change which is seen to be difficult and threatening can be made acceptable to people if they become convinced that external events are making the change imperative.

Change is also triggered and driven internally, when sufficient evidence or argument is deployed in support of a change. Changes in management priorities and preferences, reallocation of functions amongst sites or departments, problems with technology or facilities, the emergence of organizational or staff problems; all of these can become driving forces for a change.

An internal driving force

In a bank, a project was set up to review the efficiency of the information processing system. There was no direct external pressure, just a feeling at senior level that the service was not as cost-effective as it might be, and that a review was needed.

The two sources of change may support each other. In the bitumen company, the initial external stimulus was strengthened by the cost comparisons which became available once a study of alternative delivery systems was made. It became clear that the present method was not only hazardous, but was also much more expensive than some of the alternatives; when this internal evidence was supplied, the pressure for change was unstoppable.

Forces only trigger and drive change if someone sees them, recognizes they are important, is willing to act and is able to make something happen. Perceptions are therefore important. What may be a clear signal to one manager or group of staff, may be no more than a faint possibility to another. A source of information seen as authoritative and convincing by one may be seen as biased and superficial by another.

The project manager needs to ask why the project has come to life at this time – how it came to be on the management agenda. Projects only arise when somebody does something – and there may be subjective and political aspects in the situation. These will affect whether signals trigger and continue to drive the change in a powerful way, or whether they fade and disappear.

Effective management does not wait for the signals to become obvious, so that change is reactive. They sense what is about to happen, or about to become pressing, and act proactively, so as to take a lead. So the project manager may also reflect on triggers that have not yet led to change, and why these signals are being neglected.

The forces restraining change can also be assessed. They include limited energy and time. There may be so many signals that people have difficulty keeping track. Even if they see something that looks important, they may be so busy with current work that they cannot make a move on it. There may not be enough resources, there may be uncertainty or scepticism about the benefits, or opposition from

---

Internal and external restraints

A local authority had adopted a policy aimed at promoting racial equality in the provision of one of its services. Those charged with implementing the change identified these restraining forces – competing priorities, lack of resources, existing procedures (internal) – as well as a lack of understanding by the indigenous population, institutionalized racism within other organizations and presentational mistakes by some of the leaders of the ethnic minorities (external).

---

groups who see their privileges threatened. As with drivers, they can stem from both internal and external sources.

Notepad

Make a list of the forces that are driving and restraining your project, laying it out as shown in Fig. 2.1.

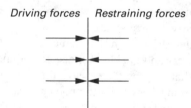

Driving forces   Restraining forces

Figure 2.1 Driving/restraining forces

- *How might you try to reduce the restraining forces?*
- *How have these forces affected the shape and priorities of the project?*
- *How can you use external pressures, trends and events to support proposals for change, in a way that is more convincing than internal pressures?*

What kind of change is it?

If people expect one kind of project but get another, they will make life difficult for those managing the change. The project manager needs to create a common, accurate perception about the kind of project being undertaken and what that means for the people affected by it. There is no such thing as a normal project. But we can describe those features which will make a project different and unique.

Project managers can then assess what these mean for their task, and how they should approach it.

Our review of the audio-diaries, and discussions with many other project managers, indicate critical features of the central project task which shape the manager's role. These are as follows:

- Core/margin.
- Novel/familiar.
- Rapid/gradual.
- Controversial/uncontroversial.

Core/margin

How close is the project to the core operating activities of the organization? At one extreme, projects are set up to bring about some change to an activity which is marginal to the business, or which is in a background, supporting role. Examples could be a project to computerize the payment of pensions to ex-employees, or one to relocate some administrative functions – useful changes, but not enhancing or threatening the survival of the business.

At the other extreme are projects whose success or failure is critical to the performance of the business. They affect core operating processes, or visible aspects of the business and its reputation. Examples include introducing a new branch accounting system in a travel agent with many retail outlets; moving a large installation within an integrated manufacturing process; or trying to change the attitude of staff to customers in an organization facing competition for the first time.

Novel/familiar

Does the change involve introducing novel, untried solutions, or established, familiar ones? Some changes apply systems or procedures which have been thoroughly tried and tested, in very similar situations. The setting is well understood, the solution is substantially known at the start of the project, and apart from the minor operating problems to be expected in any organizational activity, the project can proceed with a relatively high degree of certainty as to what the end result will look like. Examples include a plant engineering company building a standard refinery; a chain-store opening an additional retail outlet; or a company introducing an established training programme to a new part of the organization. Such projects are relatively structured and programmed.

Others depend on much learning and discovery taking place in the course of the change itself. The concepts floated are novel, and contain a high degree of uncertainty. The system or procedure has to be developed, and it is not known at the outset how the specification will be achieved. An international construction company introducing a common system into ten distinct operating businesses would be an example of this, as would a long-established organization making radical changes in its culture and ways of working. The general intention of the change is known, but those driving the project do not know how they will get there. Projects of this sort are relatively unstructured, unprogrammed, open.

Rapid/gradual

What is the pace of change? Business pressures often lead senior managers to expect change to be introduced rapidly, and so put pressure on the project manager to achieve this. Results are expected quickly, and they become impatient with requests for more time for study and design, testing, or for ensuring that training and consultation processes are done properly. Delays are seen as failures, and great store is placed on being able to see tangible evidence of progress.

Managing enthusiasm

A project to install a customer accounting system in a chain of retail outlets was being developed, and the project manager, with the equipment supplier, estimated that installation could start in twelve months. The managing director was excited by the project, saw that it would be very beneficial to the business, and demanded that the first systems be installed within six months.

Other projects are conducted at a more gradual pace, perhaps with a sequence of carefully defined phases. Pilot projects may be set up, and carefully evaluated, before the change is extended to a new site, or a new application. Planning and preparation is seen as a necessary and inevitably time-consuming part of the process, and the project manager is not under great pressure to cut corners or to produce quick results.

Controversial/uncontroversial

Will there be a fight? Some projects arouse strong disagreements. Major production or administrative reorganizations, rationalization projects or major changes in the way a service is provided are not usually seen as neutral, technical matters. They threaten established interests, who may disagree fundamentally about the direction of the change, or indeed about whether it should be undertaken at all.

Others arouse no such controversy. The change is accepted as desirable by all concerned, who willingly plan the solution. If disagreements arise, they are about means, not ends. Effort goes into the solution, not into managing deeply held disagreements. These features bring threats and opportunities as shown in Table 2.1.

Table 2.1

Feature	Threats	Opportunities
Core	Senior management pressure Penalty of failure severe Heavy responsibility	Career visibility Rewards of success Resources OK
Novel	Failure to find solution Cost and time over-run Someone else gets there first Resources underestimated	Boost to career Track record Loose budget Result hard to compare
Rapid	Pressure for quick results and corner cutting Indirect aspects ill-considered	Loose budget New job soon
Controversial	Differences harder to manage Information distorted Significant resistance	More credit for success Backing from winning side

Points to remember:

- Different people will see the same project differently. What seems like a familiar problem to one may be seen by another as novel. Such differences may reflect background and experience, or that one has considered aspects of the project the other has overlooked.
- Views will change as the project moves forward, as experience is gained, or as unexpected difficulties arise. A project that starts controversially may be managed in such a way that it ceases to be so, and becomes much less problematic.

The two most critical dimensions of the projects managed by the audio-diarists are shown in Fig. 2.2. This book is mainly directed at helping those who are managing projects which fall into quadrant 4, the projects that are core to the business, and at the same time involve the design of novel solutions. That will

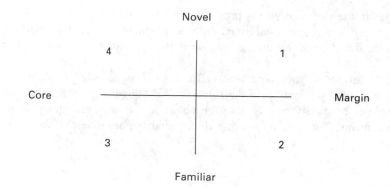

Figure 2.2 The four quadrant model of change

make it a difficult enough project to achieve on time and within budget. If, in addition, it has one or more of the other features which have been identified as critical, then the demands on the manager are that much greater.

What is the context of the change?

The study gave new insights into four features (Fig. 2.3) of the context in which the projects were taking place that affected the task of this group of managers:

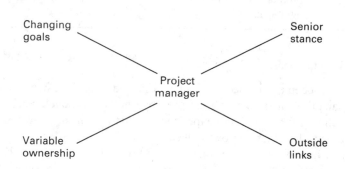

Figure 2.3 The context of the project manager

1. Changing goals

    I realized that another department was working on a similar project to ours, so I persuaded them, and senior management, to change the goals we had originally set so that both projects developed together.

2. Outside links

> The project is highly dependent on other departments changing the way they work. I don't think that was made clear enough to them (I'm not sure we fully appreciated it ourselves), they're reluctant to do it, and it has been making more unnecessary work for the staff here.

3. Variable ownership

> Senior people were quite enthusiastic about it at the start – but once the full implications became clearer, it became much harder to maintain their commitment. Whenever problems arose, they all stood back at a safe distance – nobody's willing to take responsibility for the ownership of the project.

4. Senior stance

> The Finance Department did not want the project to continue, as it conflicted with developments they had in progress. The Regional Sales Director met with the Head of Finance, but this meeting ended in a blazing row. The Regional Director then took the matter to the Chairman, and convinced him that the system would help meet corporate strategy. The Head of Finance quickly decided to go along with the project.

Sometimes these factors worked in the project manager's favour, and helped things along – more often they became major obstacles to progress, and required sustained attention from the manager. They were only partly under the manager's control, often coming into play because of the way someone else in the organization had interpreted and reacted to information or events. In any event, they represent areas of potential difficulty of which the project manager needs to be fully aware.

Changing goals

The goals of a project are shaped, and continue to evolve, in a process of dialogue between senior management and project management. In small, structured projects goals are not likely to change once the project is under way; so the issue is unlikely to concern the project manager. For the audio-diarists, managing novel projects close to the core of the business, it was another story. The goals they were expected to achieve changed, sometimes more than once, in the course of the project.

Market changes were one source of such instability:

> This project is only half-way through implementation – but already we're

introducing significant changes to cope with new areas of business which the sales and marketing people have succeeded in obtaining.

Another was a change in senior management's priorities, or a change in their thinking which opens up the terms of reference for the project:

> We've only done about 30 per cent of the scheduling devolution programme, when all of a sudden up pops this new thing, which is going to take over all my time. It's always a balance between the priorities of getting something done that is secure and can last, and doing something that is obviously coming under pressure from a very severe business need.

Wider organizational moves, or changes in other departments, also affected current projects:

> The decision to relocate the factory to new premises was taken by the management of our company after a strategic analysis of the business. A location was chosen in a new factory development near by, and the workforce assembled and briefed. The proposal was well received, and the process of identifying the equipment and facilities required in the new premises was begun.
>
> In the mean time, however, the Group as a whole had been subject to a major downturn in orders. This has meant redundancies and layoffs, and poor financial performance. So the Group Board, who had to approve the move, applied pressure for the move to be delayed. They then identified excess space in one of their existing factories, which they considered suitable for us to move to.
>
> Recently the staff have been advised of the change in plan (this has caused significant apprehension) and they foresee difficulties in moving into a large existing organization.

In these cases, clear goals had been set at the outset, but new external circumstances made it necessary to change the focus of the project. This is a feature of the world that business operates in, and which shapes the job of the project manager. Goals also changed because of failures or ambiguities in the management process (Fig. 2.4).

The lack of an identifiable corporate strategy made it hard for some project managers to fix their project goals with any degree of certainty. If project goals were left vague and uncertain at the start, they were more likely to change later.

Initial goals were sometimes based on poor information, requiring an unplanned change once the picture became clear:

> The specification of what the refinery was to produce was surprisingly difficult to prepare, as it proved impossible to get the marketing director to

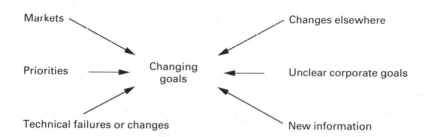

Figure 2.4 Reasons for changes in goals

be quantitative about the products he wanted to make and sell ... It was also clear that nothing had been developed for processing the by-products which would arise. All of these factors made project management very difficult, as there was a basic lack of clarity about the product range, the expected sales, or what technology would be used.

Sometimes a project was initiated by people from outside the immediate unit, without full understanding of the business – requiring changes later.

In another case:

The new corporate management backed the decision taken by the European Marketing Manager not to follow the original plan. To do this, however, the strategy was altered. In principle what they proposed was an excellent concept – but there were some technical and commercial problems associated with it.

One of the project managers had been given what he felt was a very clear brief:

The chairman and the director have clearly defined their business requirements for the system, so my remit is really quite clear.

A week later the same person reflected:

Now what's happened is that acting from one of my reports the director has decided that he is looking for a cost justification for having the system at all – especially now he's discovered there'll be a big extra cost he hadn't anticipated. For the first time, the 'do nothing' option is arising.

Notepad

- *Have the goals of your project changed during the work?*
- *What led to this change?*
- *What effects has it had on the project?*
- *How can you deal with it?*

The attitude of top management towards the change is clearly critical. They cannot give detailed guidelines, and may not even set out a clear blueprint for change. But they do need to create a climate in which initiatives around the edge of the organization are encouraged to prosper, with other changes fitting around successful ventures.

Are they visibly behind the idea of change, willing to give it the resources it needs, and with reasonable expectations of what can be achieved? How demanding are they, how tolerant of risk and delay? Will there be pressure for short cuts, or does the organization see the value of getting the change right, even if it takes longer?

The project manager needs to know who is behind the change, as a powerful sponsor or champion will see the project through the difficult times. Management at a large bank decided to establish a team whose responsibility would be to identify the bank's strategic direction on office systems. The group decided to set up a pilot project, centred on a defined 'initial users group' in order to arouse interest in the project as a whole, and thus to stimulate demand for further facilities. Discussion with the staff in the Chief Executive often revealed that there was a considerable amount of information-sharing between them, the Chairman's secretary, and the staff in the Legal and Secretarial departments. This group would be able to make good use of a shared database facility and shared word-processing, electronic mail and diary management. Being a small, cross-functional group, it was considered ideal for the first implementation of an Office System within the bank. The project manager recalled:

> The project group came to the view that the most likely supporter of the change they were proposing would be a senior secretary, who would be a frequent user of the system, and who, more importantly, had an influence over the senior manager. This proved to be the case, with the Chief Executive's secretary giving the project her support and commitment, thereby ensuring that the Chief Executive did so as well.

The champion for change – the person who will push the changes through, cajoling the doubters along and supporting the project in time of difficulty – is usually expected to be a senior manager. In the bank, this was not the case; and there is a lesson here for project managers.

The project manager should also know how powerful the person promoting the project is, and whether they can be relied on. This project manager was left exposed:

> The newly appointed Warehousing Director initially demonstrated a high degree of ownership and support for the proposal. Although this arrangement

worked well in the early stages, the Director lost interest in giving the scheme his personal attention, preferring to concentrate on matters of 'strategy', and allowing 'urgent matters' to take precedence.

It is also prudent to assess if any members of senior management are opposed to the project, and how sustained that is likely to be. A project may run counter to the basic values and beliefs of some senior managers, or threaten powerful interests. If significant groups or individuals are intent on undermining or disrupting the change, the management problems will be markedly different from those experienced in less controversial changes.

A project manager in a public utility had been told by senior management to assess the feasibility of a computerized maintenance planning system. He assessed the options, and concluded that a system based on personal computers, linked to the mainframe computer, would give the best financial return. He went on:

> So I became the promoter of this option. The people who were least in favour of it were the management services people, the computer people; perhaps they saw it as a weakening of their power base. They had a vested interest in mainframes, and they didn't want a stand alone option, a PC option, to be considered at all. They were a bit surprised that I had even considered it, and their response was a bit like 'if you won't go for the mainframe system, you won't get anything'. That gave rise to quite a considerable discussion.

Clearly the project manager will need support from senior management here, if his position is not to be undermined.

The culture of the organization – the prevailing pattern of values, beliefs, expected ways of working – will affect how the change is perceived. Is the change consistent with this style, or is it seen as a threat? Large-scale changes, at the core of the business, often require basic rethinking by senior managers about the way the company does business. Most companies have developed a set of shared, usually unwritten, beliefs which guide their decisions. If the company has been successful these beliefs will have a powerful influence on senior manager's attitudes – since they have worked well.

Such beliefs will shape the way a change project is seen by senior managers. They may find it hard to see or accept the signals which triggered the change, if these run counter to previous experience. They may also encourage a preference for changes which are closer to current practice, over those which involve radical departures from a previously winning formula.

The project task will be materially affected by the ability of the organization to cope with the kind of change proposed. Does it have adequate procedures and mechanisms for setting strategy – not only for initiating a change project, but for

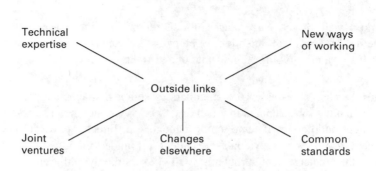

Figure 2.5   Reasons for managing outside links

managing the wider consequences which may be set off? Is the overall structure likely to be able to cope with the processes of change, by having a relatively integrated form, or will a segmented, divided structure inhibit change? Are senior managers able to derive lessons from similar change projects, and how does their experience of similar changes colour their reaction to the current change?

Notepad

Use these headings to assess the stance of senior managers towards your project:

- *Project champion. Who? How committed? Their status? Their future?*
- *Opposition. Where from? On what grounds? Overt or latent? Sustainable?*
- *Culture. How would you describe it? Threatened by, or consistent with, the change? Will it help or hinder your change programme?*
- *Ability to change. Are people in the organization used to the kind of change being introduced, or is it an unusual event? Are there established mechanisms and procedures for managing the processes of change?*
- *Top management attitude. Supportive? Indifferent? Willing to pay the price for a good job?*

Outside links

Many of the projects handled by the audio-diarists depended on outside links. They needed the cooperation of people from outside their own area, who were not necessarily as committed to the proposed changes as those managing them.

Projects may need technical expertise or resources from other departments, suppliers or sub-contractors (Fig. 2.5). A small oil-refining company embarked on a project to build a new plant. They lacked the experience to design the process, or the engineering of the plant, so they decided to work with an engineering contractor. This link worked well, but severe difficulties were caused to the project later when the work being done by a piping sub-contractor was found to be unsatisfactory, causing a critical delay.

The same company suffered dramatically when it received an unexpected announcement that there would be a three-month interruption in its supply of crude oil; alternatives were not as suitable, and caused technical and marketing difficulties:

> We were negligent in our approach to our suppliers, in that we did not adequately sustain a relationship with them, to the extent that they did not advise us of their impending refinery closure.

Management at an electronics company decided to enter a new market, and concluded that the only way to acquire the expertise it needed was to join a smaller company already skilled in this field:

> We were to provide the technology and manufacturing capacity to the partner, while they would take a team of our engineers and work together on refining their system and design tools.

A project based in one department may need others to agree to changes in their ways of working. The leader of the team designing a new product in the electronics company found:

> Other product groups were not prepared to alter their design methods in a way that would make it easier for our product to fit into the overall package offered to the customer. This made it less likely that our project would be successful. What was needed was to get other groups to design their circuits on compatible principles, so that all the building blocks would be able to fit together.

Some projects inevitably involve working across boundaries (Fig. 2.6). The

An outside link

A project to install an automated record system in a hospital laboratory depended on information about the sample and the patient to be available to the clerical staff in a specific form, so that they could enter it into the machine. This depended on the clinicians who had sent the sample, and who were located in hospitals throughout Scotland, being willing to change the way they filled in the paperwork, and to follow a standard procedure. They could not be relied on to do that, so an additional step had to be introduced at the laboratory to 'translate' the data.

There are three types of links between departments or functions.

Pooled: little sharing of information, with departments working independently on their part of the task, with limited coordination needed, achievable by standards, rules and procedures.

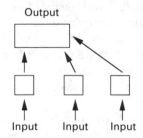

Sequential: departments linked in series, with the output from one being the input to the next; coordination by plans and schedules.

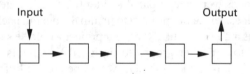

Reciprocal: work and information flowing back and forth between departments until the task is complete; coordination by group meetings and mutual agreement.

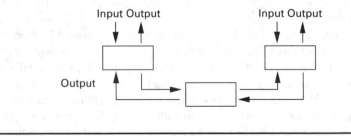

Figure 2.6 Forms of dependencies between departments

project manager has to find ways to link facilities, and the interests that go with them, in a joint project that is part of a wider exercise. A manager in a company manufacturing in five European sites saw that their competitive performance could be improved if the order scheduling system could be improved. This matched customer requirements to the facilities at the different production locations, each of which was responsible for part of the range of equipment that would typically make up an order. He would need to get all to agree to a new system.

Changes elsewhere may trigger change in a project already under way. A Scottish subsidiary of a company based in the United States had begun a project to introduce computer-aided drawing equipment. The parent company later decided to do the same, but with a different, and incompatible, system:

> It was therefore decided to install a system of the same basic type at the Scottish plant as this would benefit inter-company communications, and it would also provide a common library of parts.

New hardware and software had to be acquired to run the system.

Projects often have to be designed so that they are compatible with industry standards, either on a national or an international scale. These include not only health or safety standards, but also those covering documentation or quality procedures.

Notepad

- *Which of these situations in Fig. 2.6 best describes the operation into which your project is being introduced?*
- *Mark your project, and the relevant departments, on a picture like those shown.*
- *How will the project affect those other departments?*
- *What are they expected to do differently during and after the project?*

Managing links with other departments is an element of any manager's job, so this is nothing new. Separate functions acquire different cultures and ways of working. Some may be receptive to change, and keen to move ahead quickly; others need longer to adjust. They have different priorities, reflecting their part of the business, and other demands on them.

The project manager is competing for their time and commitment against other demands and priorities. Moreover, the project manager usually has to manage them with little direct power and authority.

Why are outside links becoming a bigger issue?

- **Technical developments:** developments in information technology make it possible to put in computer systems linking geographically separate operations, including those of other organizations.

- **Joint ventures:** political, legal and economic developments encourage joint ventures with other organizations, often in other countries.
- **Larger organizations:** recognition of the benefits of developing potentially compatible systems across large organizations, rather than isolated ones.

So the need to manage different functional perspectives is likely to be present from the start of the project.

Such links are easier to handle if good working relationships have been established in the past, and if the project manager works to maintain these during the project. This is helped if adequate communication procedures have been created:

> Communication, especially in an international setting, is extremely critical. Not only can strategy be understood, but technical problems can be solved rather than prolonged. Also undesired political situations are more likely to arise due to poor communications.

Notepad

- *Which functions or units does your project depend on?*
- *What do you expect of them?*
- *How good are your communication links with them? How strong is the relationship?*
- *How important is the project to them?*

Variable ownership

Projects need sustained commitment, support and a sense of ownership from powerful backers in the organization. These audio-diarists' accounts showed how this was needed both from top management and from other functional heads, whose support was needed to help the project along. It matters in the tangible sense of providing manager and staff with a sense that their work is recognized and valued in the business:

> Management responsibility for the new system was placed mainly on the electrical controls manager, although some responsibility was also placed upon the individual department managers who would use the system within their own departments. The range of these responsibilities was vague, and there was no clear division of responsibility until the equipment had been introduced.

Where a change is seen as coming in from outside, the project manager needs to develop a sense of ownership and commitment towards the project amongst those who may be indifferent towards it. This is illustrated by the manager in the early stages of putting in a company-wide system, in a business which had already had a lot of change:

> I feel some of the managers are a bit stunned at the amount of change – there are so many changes taking place, they are more or less numb, and this is simply another change which they are just going to have to take on board. The result is that they are somewhat 'passive neutral', so when I try to talk to them about their requirements, the response is along the lines of 'you tell me'.

It is comparatively easy for other managers to express a generalized interest, to give vague expressions of support:

> It was noted by the Electric Controls Manager that most departments only paid lip-service to the installation of CAD. There was no real commitment to its use, since they had not asked for it.

In some areas that may be enough – all the project manager may need from them is that they do not oppose things.

But others need stiffer backing – public support or the provision of resources. One of the audio-diarists had difficulty getting his manager to show support, because of other priorities:

> The development director to whom I reported had significant problems in his own area in the States. Little time could be devoted to interfacing with the UK. Part of the reason for this was the size of the organization reporting to him. He had literally no time to devote to strategic direction, and the role was mainly firefighting. As a result, progress in the development activity was minimal.

The project managers often needed to build commitment and a sense of ownership amongst those with no initial interest in the success of the task. In one case:

> The significant point here is that this project has been driven by head office, actually the chairman and one of his directors, rather than by the operational side. It will open up day-to-day operational performance to senior management . . . so operational management are a little bit dubious at this stage.

But the scheme depended on the active support of the latter group. Their initial reaction showed clearly that, so far as they were concerned, ownership still remained at the top of the organization. Unless the project manager was able to develop a sense of ownership amongst the staff in the areas who would need to operate it, it was clear that no sustainable changes would occur.

The depth of support (or opposition) within a group is also worth reviewing. A senior manager may, for example, express strong support and commitment to the project, but be unable to deliver the necessary backing from the staff.

Conversely, opposition may be confined to the top, with the staff keen to go ahead.

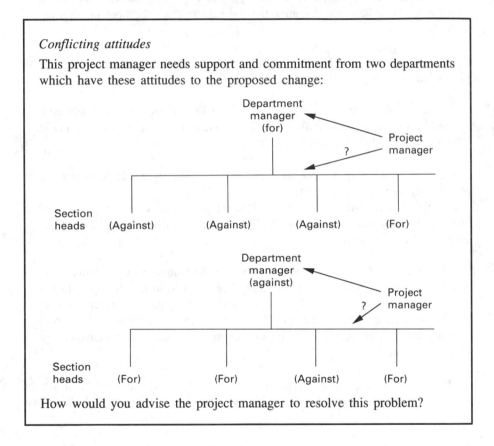

Conflicting attitudes

This project manager needs support and commitment from two departments which have these attitudes to the proposed change:

How would you advise the project manager to resolve this problem?

A manager may filter information, preventing his or her colleagues from having enough knowledge to become committed:

It was apparent that X did not communicate the main issues which arose during the course of the project to the Board. For example, when we reviewed capital requirements with the designers, it was some weeks later that I discovered the rest of the Board had not been told of our decision to reduce capacity in order to reduce capital cost. While the Board ostensibly retained responsibility for the project, in fact, they tended to be uninvolved . . .

Support or commitment can also be intrusive or disruptive, if it is seen by a project manager to be becoming an interference in *their* responsibilities – as when a senior director suddenly started taking a close interest in a project, and imposing his own ideas on a project manager.

A useful idea here may be to think in terms of 'degrees of commitment'. The attitude of people towards a project can be anywhere along a scale from outright opposition, through lukewarm interest, to fully committed support. An important job is to assess where key groups really are on this scale, and then to decide how to move them up the scale of commitment, if that is necessary for the project.

Notepad

- *Select three of the functions you identified in the previous notepad.*
- *Where would you place them on the scale in Fig. 2.7, in terms of their degree of commitment to the project?*
- *How sure are you of their commitment?*

Vigorous and sustained opposition	Sceptical and reluctant to help but may be persuaded	Indifferent, will not help but will not oppose	Moderately interested but not keen to offer support	Very keen, genuinely willing to back it tangibly

Figure 2.7   Degrees of commitment to a change

Building and sustaining ownership is made more difficult by the problems of goals and links. Wide links or dependencies mean genuine commitment has to be obtained from a correspondingly wide range of functions and levels. Shifting goals can lead to the erosion of commitments already established.

Where are the pitfalls?

Project managers can assess where the trouble is most likely to arise, and what that means for how they need to manage the change, by using the checklist shown in Table 2.2. It brings together the features of change projects discussed above. Projects can be reviewed against these features, by placing a tick at the point on each of the scales which most accurately describes the project. High scores indicate where trouble is most likely to arise. Later chapters of this book show how these features can be handled more confidently and effectively.

A low total score suggests a problem with relatively clear boundaries, a

The setting

Table 2.2   Project profile tool

Significance:	Margin	1 2 3 4 5	Core
Solution:	Familiar	1 2 3 4 5	Novel
Pace:	Gradual	1 2 3 4 5	Rapid
Intentions:	Uncontroversial	1 2 3 4 5	Controversial
Changing goals:	Rare/minor	1 2 3 4 5	Often/major
Senior stance:	Supportive	1 2 3 4 5	Unsupportive
Outside links:	Few	1 2 3 4 5	Many
Sense of ownership:	High	1 2 3 4 5	Low

relatively clear set of agreed objectives, and where the steps to be taken to achieve the result are fairly predictable. A change of this sort is often referred to as being 'hard', 'structured' or 'bounded', or perhaps a 'difficulty'. It may be a challenging and demanding result to achieve; but it is concerned with reasonably well-known issues.

A high total score suggests a more ambiguously defined activity, with disagreement over objectives, and little certainty about how to achieve them. The change is relatively 'soft', 'unstructured', 'unbounded': a 'mess'. It will raise different problems from those experienced in managing a project which is a 'difficulty'. There will be more uncertainty, more changes to plan, more political activity, more compromise. The route to be followed will not be clear.

Do people share the same view of the kind of task they are working on? The project manager will be very vulnerable if others see the change in structured terms, if in fact it is ambiguous and political. They may then use the wrong approach, expect a fairly straightforward activity, and become impatient with delay while differences are resolved.

Change management is about introducing some structure into an unbounded, unstructured problem. It is about turning an apparently insoluble mess into a soluble difficulty, by reducing the uncertainties to manageable proportions. This can be done by gathering information that will help reduce or eliminate successive areas of uncertainty. By assessing the level of uncertainty in respective areas of the project, it may be possible to see those which can be dealt with now, and those which need still to remain ambiguous.

This understanding needs to be shared by others connected with the project. Once the the project manager is clear about the nature of the task, it becomes easier to pass that to others, so as to develop a common picture.

Personal checkpoints

- Write out on a couple of sheets of paper what kind of project it is that you are managing, using the frameworks above.
- Identify on the paper those areas that will cause you most difficulty.
- Think who it would be useful to discuss this with tomorrow, to gain their views and advice.
- Write down how this task will differ from others you have been involved in.
- Make notes showing how you intend to manage this project differently from previous jobs.

3

The job of the project manager

What project managers do and the skills they use

People handling a major change need a clear picture of what the main activities will be, and the skills they will need to use. This chapter sets out what the managers in our study said they were doing, and what skills they appeared to be using. A key feature of the job is clearly that of influencing other people, using a range of process and political skills – skills not usually linked with project management.

The activities are familiar aspects of the management process, and the competences needed are relatively easy to acquire and improve. They can also be used to support any or all of the three perspectives on the change management process which have been identified in earlier studies. They are thus a powerful set of tools for the manager to have available. The themes are as follows:

Models of change.
Key activities of project managers.
A new emphasis in project management.

Models of change

A great deal of the advice given to those responsible for managing change projects is based on the concept of the project life cycle. This approach argues that success in managing a project depends on the clear definition and statement of four dimensions – objectives, responsibilities, deadlines and budgets. This implies that the project manager needs to be skilled in the substance or content of the change, and in techniques of monitoring and control.

The many approaches of this type are sometimes referred to as 'rational-linear' models of change. They are based on the assumption that planned change in organizations unfolds in a logically sequenced manner, that people do what is expected of them to complete the project, that deviations are noticed and corrected. For some projects, and for some parts of other projects, these assumptions are reasonable; where that is the case, rational-linear models are valuable sources of guidance to the manager introducing change. If the assumptions are not correct, the manager who relies on this approach will not succeed.

A second well-established set of approaches to the management of change are the 'participative' models. These emphasize the benefits of establishing a sense of ownership of the change amongst those whose support will be needed, or who will have to live with the change when it is implemented. Many prescriptions have been offered to achieve that sense of ownership, and to overcome resistance. Typically these include involving those affected by the change in the design of solutions; consulting widely about possible options; ensuring that information is widely communicated; providing imaginative training and support; and ensuring that conflicts or disagreements are openly and skilfully dealt with.

Participative approaches to change are consistent with democratic values and beliefs, and it is easy to agree that those managing change should seek to follow these prescriptions. However, since change projects regularly run into difficulties, there must be something wrong with the easy prescription. One possibility is that although the remedies sound easy, they are in practice difficult and time-consuming to put into effect. The project manager able to handle all the dimensions of a participative change process is rare, especially when under pressure from a range of other demands on their time and energy.

A second reason is that in some situations participative approaches are inappropriate or unworkable. Where there is wide agreement on how to proceed, or where the practical scope for consultation to change matters is limited, then to go through the motions of participative management is dishonest and time-wasting. If there is wide and fundamental disagreement from some parties to the change, participation can lead to the change being blocked – in which case those pushing the change are unlikely to engage in it.

In other words, participative approaches assume that a sensitive approach by reasonable people will result in the willing acceptance and implementation of change. For some changes, and in some organizations, that assumption will be correct – in which case the approach will be a relevant source of guidance to the project manager. However, as with the 'rational-linear' models of change, if the assumptions do not fit reality, the guidance will be misleading.

A third set of perspectives on the change process is one that is more firmly based on observation of the messy realities of organizational life, and recognizes that significant change will be a technically complex task, and will often be seen as a challenge or threat to established interests. There are likely to be many different interests involved, possibly pulling in different directions, and usually pursuing personal as well as organizational goals. The practical implication of this is that in situations where there is significant disagreement about ends and means, and where resources are scarce, important change projects are likely to be much more difficult to manage than is implied by either the rational or participative models of change.

In politically charged situations, effective management of the project is likely to require the exercise of political skills, as well as those of problem-solving and participation. Those managing the change will need to be sensitive to the power and influence of key individuals in the organization, and to how the pattern of influence will be altered by the change. They are likely to have to be able and willing to negotiate and sell ideas to indifferent or sceptical colleagues, to filter information in order to change perceptions, and to undertake a variety of activities to make the change seem legitimate within the organization. The skills are in some ways similar to those prescribed in the participative approach, but they are directed towards building credibility, marshalling support and blocking opposition on behalf of the project as a whole, rather than to dealing directly with the individuals or groups affected by the change.

Key activities of project managers

Each project is different, and takes place in a unique organizational setting, so the job of every project manager will also be unique. Nevertheless, we can learn from the experience of others who have implemented major change. The audio-diaries kept by the project managers give many insights into the key activities in which they were engaged. The clues were comments about things they had done, or that others had done, which had affected the progress or otherwise of the project. Sometimes, too, their comments implied that something had not been done which should have been – and such examples are taken into account as well.

The authors worked through the diary accounts several times independently, and then compared their conclusions about the main activities being undertaken by the project managers. In addition, we included a section on this in the questionnaire survey. Respondents were asked to review a list of skills which they believed had been useful in the management of significant changes. The list had been compiled both from the analysis of the audio-diary records, from discussions with other project managers, and from other publications on the topic. There were thirty-two items in the list, and respondents were asked to indicate, for each one, whether they felt that item was 'very helpful', 'somewhat helpful' or 'not at all helpful'.

The following eight items were rated most often as being 'very helpful':

1. Securing agreement on goals.
2. Ensuring departments know what is expected.
3. Securing resources.
4. Improving communication between those involved.
5. Ensuring staff understand the reasons for change.

6. Visualizing how it all fits together.
7. Clarifying roles early.
8. Ensuring people see benefits to them.

As expected, the results of the survey broadly confirm the picture built up from the diary records.

We therefore combined the results from the diaries and the survey to produce this list of the key activities of the project managers who took part in this study:

1. Shaping goals: setting or receiving overall objectives and directions, interpreting them, reacting to changes in them, clarifying the problem and setting boundaries to it.
2. Obtaining resources: identifying them, negotiating for their release, retaining them, managing their effective use.
3. Building roles and structures: clarifying and modifying their own, and those of other functions.
4. Establishing good communications: linking the diverse groups or individuals contributing to the project, to obtain their support and commitment.
5. Seeing the whole picture: taking a helicopter view, managing time and other resources, anticipating reactions from stakeholders, spotting links and unexpected events.
6. Moving things forward: taking action and risks to keep the project going, especially through difficult phases.

The emphasis differed between projects, but taken together these were the areas that needed effective handling if the project was to succeed. It is also worth noting that the focus of the activities identified was consistent with the three models of the change process outlined in the previous section. In some instances the activities were clearly undertaken in a 'problem-solving' mode – to sort out a non-contentious issue before the next stage of the project could move ahead. In others, we observe the manager doing something which is clearly consistent with the prescriptions of the participative approach to project management, while in others again, it is clear that work was being done to manage a political situation.

Shaping goals

The changes frequently took place in a volatile setting, requiring the project managers to spend time clarifying what the goals should be, obtaining commitment and reacting to changes.

Some managers came to the project after the overall goals had been set by senior management. They had little scope to debate or change. For example, a local authority decided to change the pattern of domestic refuse collection throughout the city, so as to achieve a 20 per cent cut in labour costs, with no detrimental effect on the service provided to the public. The project manager assigned explains:

> The Director of Cleansing requested help from the Controller of Management Services to implement this change. I was assigned as project leader, my role being to lead a team of management services officers to review present methods, plan and implement new schedules, and monitor the effects.

Similarly, top management at the steel company described earlier had no doubt that they wanted a large piece of plant relocated away from its present site, as part of a strategic reorganization of the business, and that it had to be done in a very short period. How that was to be achieved, within the time available, was left to the project manager who was put in charge of guiding the transfer. The role of these project leaders in relation to goals was consistent with the problem-solving approach. They needed to ensure they understood what was needed, and that this was equally well defined to team members.

Contrast this with the manager recruited to a refinery project. Senior management had developed the broad concept of the project (to build a new refinery), and then recruited him to provide a specification, and to manage the whole project. Difficulties soon became apparent:

> The specification of what the refinery was to produce was surprisingly difficult, as it proved impossible to get the marketing director to specify the products that he wanted to make and sell. I was surprised to find that the basic technology for an important step in the process had not been finalized ... hence even at the project inception there were several technology areas that had not been defined ... all of this made project management very difficult, because it was starting from a lack of clarity about what the product range had to be, what were the expected sales forecasts, and what technology was to be used.

This lack of initial clarity by senior management, and the inability of the project manager (who was new to the company and had relatively limited authority) to persuade senior management to agree on targets, brought difficulty to the project throughout its life.

In other cases, project managers themselves had initiated the project. They had a strong influence on goals and direction:

> It was a yawning gap, and something had to be done. So I volunteered to pull together a group of people from across our other facilities, and put our thoughts on paper ... We gathered a group of people who had a vision of

what the order scheduling was about, and how it could be done in the future. After a few months we had the bare bones of a plan, and I began a round of presentations to plant staffs, and to management, describing the problem and suggesting a way forward.

Although the manager in this case was initiating the idea, he would only succeed if he was able to get support and approval from the top. He needed that not only to back his own use of resources, but also to have senior backing for the change when he needed to persuade other managers to give their commitment – which some were reluctant to do.

An example of goal-setting being carried out in a way that reflected to some degree the participative approach occurred in a company where a team had been set up to design a new electronic product. The team had met several setbacks, but in due course:

Following a period of some difficulty in the business, a new director prepared new strategies. These would be very attractive to my group, which had experienced a lot of unwelcome changes in the previous two years. It was agreed that my group would immediately become familiar with the new tools. The director travelled back to the UK with me so that the new strategies could be sold to local engineers. Obviously there was initially a feeling of 'Here we go again, another change', 'What lies in store for us this time?' But as the meeting progressed, attitudes changed and became very positive.

Notepad

How much scope do you have for shaping the goals in your project? Were they:

- *Already set and defined?*
- *Set in broad terms, leaving you to detail them?*
- *Up to you to propose?*

Obtaining resources

Project managers in this study spent a great deal of time fighting for resources – an issue taken for granted in rational-linear approaches to project management. It was difficult to specify what these would be at the outset, and whatever was agreed then was liable to change. The manager of a product development project in the electronics industry commented:

The new Director has altered the policy of aiming to offer the new device to a lot of customers. Perhaps the major mistake when the change was initiated was that management underestimated the task to set up this particular facility. Now it has been realized that great resources will have to be deployed to achieve this.

The most difficult situation arose when the manager depended on specific types of staff, who were currently doing other work for other managers. The latter had to be persuaded to give them up. Projects often needed staff who were competent in the operational area concerned, *and* who possessed skills and attitudes relevant to the project. Such people were scarce and their managers were usually reluctant to release them, to the detriment of their own priorities and interests:

> I personally started to recruit the staff required for the refinery, starting with the current refinery manager who was to be my assistant for the commissioning period. An important feature of the project was to weld the staff together as a team . . . One disappointment (and, I believe, a significant factor in the project), was that just before commissioning, the manager of the pilot plant development was transferred to another job. He had been promised to me at the project inception, and I had designed him into the working operation.

The same man also commented:

> One of the major drawbacks in my view was that the commissioning staff could have been augmented by skilled professionals from within the company, but this was denied me as project manager. This threw a heavy strain on myself and my assistant. It put me in a position of high stress, from the point of view that I knew the future of the whole company rested upon the successful outcome of the project, and engendered high physical stress imposed by very long working hours.

The promoter of a European-wide project invested much time and effort in the pursuit of the necessary staff:

> I understand [his] circumstances having worked there before. So I have agreed with him that we will put together a plan to augment the materials and planning resource at that plant. I will try to provide him with the support for [his own needs, and for] this long-term programme . . . I have asked the European manufacturing manager to pull together all the manufacturing managers in each of the plants . . . and to indicate to them the nature of the work that needs to be done, and the criticality of this work. This may or may not be enough to secure the necessary support and resource . . . to do the prescribed work.

A major and continuing activity was then that of identifying requirements, and persuading those with the power to do so to release what they needed.

Notepad

- *What resources have you needed to secure for your project?*
- *Where have you obtained them?*
- *Can you think of more unusual sources?*

Building roles and structures

Project roles were often expressed in very general terms, leaving a great deal of scope for interpretation and definition – a theme that features strongly in rational-linear approaches to project management. Sometimes the manager had created the role himself:

> I realized there was a yawning gap in the market for what we wanted to do. So I gathered a few people from around Europe together, and I volunteered to pull the ideas together in a paper.

The roles and responsibilities of other departments or contributors to the project also needed to be defined:

> There was some responsibility placed upon the individual department managers, but they were vague and there was no clear division of responsibilities until much later.

In other projects, building a satisfactory role ran into deeper difficulties. One manager experienced severe political limitations in his role:

> My role was not properly set up, and clearly it was my mistake that I would be subordinate to the Board, and not a member of it. In hindsight I really needed to operate at the highest level to carry the necessary 'clout', and also to keep the Board itself properly informed.

This was a common theme in the diary accounts – with some indicating difficulty in the area, others attributing the success of the project to the way this had been handled. Clarifying roles is of course a common managerial activity, but was made difficult by the setting in which projects were being carried out. The more volatile this was, and the wider the pattern of links and dependencies, the more difficult it became to establish clear, mutually supportive roles.

A closely related activity was that of establishing structures to link the different parts of the project together, especially to build reporting links to top management and to establish the legitimacy of the project team.

Reporting links

The benefits of establishing close links to top management was provided by an office automation project in a multinational company. The capital cost of what was proposed was not great in terms of the group's overall capital expenditure, and the project was to be implemented in phases, so the business risks were fairly limited. It would have been relatively easy for the project to have gone ahead with Board approval, but with very little subsequent interest on their part.

The project manager took the view, however, that there would be benefits in ensuring that the Board was kept informed about what was happening, and secured the support of a technologically aware director, to provide the Board with regular factual reports on progress. This not only served to counter any damaging rumours about difficulties or delay; it provided the basis for a Board that was receptive to later proposals of a similar kind, that allowed the business as a whole to benefit from later applications of information technology.

The role of the sponsor of the project is also critical if the project is to get the sustained backing and support that it needs. The project manager needs to build and exploit a supportive relationship with whoever is in the role of sponsor. This includes ensuring that the project is properly established by top management. The manager of the European order scheduling programme felt a major step forward had been taken when he was able to record:

A number of interesting things have happened. I personally have been legitimized by my division's management team as the Customer Service and Order Fulfilment Manager. I have also been legitimized as the European Programme Manager for order scheduling. Of the seventeen part-timers who started on this project, we now have at least ten of them committed full time to the programme. The process of engagement has begun.

These are not new management themes – but they clearly occupied these project managers, and were difficult to handle in volatile projects with extensive links to other functions. They show that the managers were having to exercise political skills, as well as those of a problem-solving and participative nature.

Establishing good communications

The project managers typically needed to get things done with the cooperation of groups or functions over whom they had little or no formal authority. They had to engage in an intense communication process, using a wide variety of methods: clarifying goals and ensuring they were understood; making the case for adequate resources; presenting ideas and proposals to senior managers, operators, suppliers; listening to ideas, picking up signs of trouble; and so on. Many of their accounts showed them being active in building and maintaining good communication links with those involved in the project.

Sometimes the activity fitted the problem-solving approach to project management. The technical problems of good communications were especially visible where widely dispersed international programmes were concerned:

> The local team were suffering increased frustration from the difficulties with the system, and poor communications. When tasks were thought to be complete, the UK engineers would find that systems software had been updated. This could mean redoing the work – there was a lack of procedures to communicate changes to the appropriate parties.

Another man commented:

> As most of the design elements originated in the USA, it was physically difficult to get the relevant information necessary to understand sufficiently well what needed to be done.

Even projects that were less physically separate needed, for example, to sustain good relations with suppliers, so as to be up to date with changes in *their* facilities which could have implications for the job.

Others communicated with staff as part of a participative approach to the task. In the course of his account of a project which had got into difficulty, the manager described his response:

> How best to tackle this? I decided that again I wanted to communicate with everybody who may be involved with this system, talk to them, try to identify the potential benefits ... so that we can have a full reflection of the management's requirements, both present and future.

Later he reflected on the process:

> I have now had a few meetings, and there are more to go, with the various managers, to discuss benefits. We are in the process of gathering costs. So having got these, I can collate them and submit a report to the director, and

from there a decision will be taken on whether to go ahead or not. I like to think that ... by going out and talking to these guys, and constructively managing the thing in a sense which includes their contribution, there's an increasing awareness of this system, and how it can radically change their ways of working.

The project team was another focus for this aspect of the communication process. The managers generally recognized the need, once a team had been created, to spend time on maintaining it, and on keeping its commitment and interest.

Very soon after the division was established, the new manager called for a one-week brainstorming/team-building session in Geneva. All managers of the various groups participated ... As a result of this meeting, relationships were established, and objectives agreed. The manager felt excited about the possibility of getting his team involved in state-of-the-art design developments.

Passing on accurate information (aware of how fast bad news could drive down morale), providing information about impending or possible changes, ensuring the team remembered what they had achieved, as well as their current problems; all indicated that this group of project managers regarded communication as a major element in the effective management of projects.

Others had to communicate with departments which were indifferent or hostile to the project, but whose commitment was needed. Managers spent time and energy (emotional as well as physical) putting the case for the project, persuading people to release resources or to change working practices. They had to do this to people who were often sceptical or indifferent – in other divisions, or in other countries. They wanted to sell the project as they saw it, but were also aware of the need to listen, to test reaction and to take this into account in deciding how to move the task forward.

Seeing the whole picture

This phrase reflects comments indicating the need for the manager, especially in a relatively segmented organization, to be able to rise above the project, and take a broad view of where it was going. They had to look ahead, to anticipate events with implications for their job. Phrases such as 'You need to have eyes in the back of your head' and 'You need to be a mind reader' were often used.

Sometimes this activity was directed at the subject matter of the project. For example, a project can benefit from similar activities elsewhere. That work often goes on in parallel, without either party knowing what the other is doing:

I found out that one of the business units was developing a system very similar to our own – but hadn't thought to tell anybody.

Others found that building an awareness of developments in other areas of the organization helped to smooth the way for their own project (Fig. 3.1):

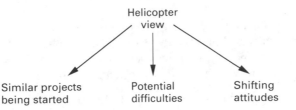

Figure 3.1 Benefits of taking a helicopter view

I met X briefly in the corridor yesterday and mentioned a few things we hope to discuss with them soon. He seemed to be thinking along the same lines, and some of the things they are already doing with other departments are very similar to what we want. We can now both be thinking about it at the same time.

Taking a helicopter view helped managers to spot difficulties. One realized that the system that senior management wanted him to install had been developed in another part of the business, for their unique purposes, and would not be easy to transfer. In another case a man wanted to press for the regrading of a post – but realized that the easy, short-term decision could jeopardize a longer-term reorganization that he was planning. A final example was the project manager who observed that, although a system was technically satisfactory, relations with the partner in this joint-venture were beginning to go wrong, and that this was likely to place serious limitations on later developments.

Wide vision also helped managers to spot difficulties of a process nature – of the way in which the project was being handled, and of people's attitudes towards it. One man saw that the difficulties a project was experiencing were being made worse by rumours. The engineers had maintained contact with their counterparts in the United States after an initial training exercise and now the problems and difficulties were being fed back to the United Kingdom via the grapevine. As only the bad news filters through, things appeared worse than they were. Another realized that morale was low because of changes elsewhere, and feared that unless he did something, staff would leave.

These examples give a sense of project managers overseeing a wide range of events relevant to their project. They show the value of keeping a distance from day-to-day events, so as to be able to spot political as well as technical issues emerging. Maintaining wide awareness appears essential if projects in a volatile environment are to be controlled and kept on track.

Moving things forward

The managers in the survey generally kept things moving – often in the face of considerable difficulty and uncertainty. They did this with a mixture of flexibility and persistent determination. They took advantage of opportunities as they came up – and dealt promptly with delays and potential problems:

- A man was puzzling about how to tackle a problem, so he contacted colleagues in other organizations to gather ideas – a successful application of a well-known problem-solving technique.
- A change in plan seemed imminent, so the manager communicated again with everybody who was likely to be involved so as to have a full picture of their requirements – as any writer on participative management would recommend.
- A new director was appointed, so the project manager quickly made arrangements to go and see him, so as to enhance the power of the coalition supporting the project.

Difficulties were confronted rather than being allowed to drag on:

> I realized the attitude of one section head towards the changes was negative, that it was clear to all staff, and that he was unable to curb his feelings. We had to face up to this – so we had some valuable counselling and training sessions, and his attitude improved considerably.

A common problem in projects involving many functions or different members of staff is that different areas will be able and ready to move at different times. It is highly unlikely that all will be in a positive and willing frame of mind at the same time – to wait for that would slow a project beyond reason. The managers in this study clearly kept things moving by being flexible – moving in the areas which were most likely to be receptive, holding back on areas of difficulty. This allowed momentum to be maintained, successes demonstrated, and perhaps resistance to begin to crumble.

That patience, sensitivity and sense of timing – knowing when to push, and when to hold back – was balanced by a deep determination to succeed, especially on the longer, more complex, projects. The bigger the change, the more scope for delay and disappointment; and it was striking how often a willingness to stick at it, to refuse to give up in the face of technical problems, opposition, indifference, came through in the project accounts:

> A lesson I received from this project was that it is absolutely essential to

maintain one's stability and equilibrium, and not to give way to despair when things go wrong. One has to maintain a positive, outward face and smile at all times when things are deteriorating. If one perseveres then, eventually, things *do* get better.

In many ways system design is now going through the very same as happened to some product design in its early days. An individual or group of individuals need to go out on a limb with an idea, and be able to articulate that to a wider audience before they can get any interest and support to go forward ... At the moment what's happening is that I'm having to push very hard.

Project managers clearly needed determination and persistence. One very novel project, with the system being developed in conjunction with the supplier, ran into technical difficulties. A member of the team commented:

They could have decided at that stage that this was too much to handle, and gone back to the earlier method. However, I think because of the personalities, because of their determination to succeed and diversify, they kept going.

Managers were also helped in moving things forward by the ambiguity of their roles. These were often set out in vague terms; and since the ownership of projects was itself often unclear, those managing the change frequently had few constraints placed upon them.

A new emphasis in project management

The activities outlined in the previous section

shaping goals
obtaining resources
building roles and structures
establishing good communications
seeing the whole picture
moving things forward

are largely concerned with trying to influence others to act in a particular way. They are not the activities of the careful analyst, working out precisely the best solution to the project. They are the activities of an entrepreneur, determined to get things done within an often hostile, indifferent or highly political setting. They are typically operating across established functional or departmental boundaries, and working with a wide variety of different people, who have their own interests to pursue.

They therefore have very little formal authority – yet the key part of their job is to influence others to do certain things. To be successful, they have to be able to use a wide range of methods, especially those drawing on political and interpersonal skills. Such skills (such as communicating, negotiating, team-building, creating ownership) are quite different from those which figured in the original training of most project managers.

These conclusions were borne out by many discussions with managers involved with change projects. A frequent comment was that conventional guidance on project management placed too much emphasis on rational approaches, and the design of technically sound solutions. For some projects that will be sufficient – but the more novel the project, and the more volatile the context, the less likely that becomes.

Experienced project managers were clear that they needed more guidance on the implementation aspects – well aware that successful projects require high levels of commitment and imagination from those affected. This can be gained in part by the effective use of participative techniques – taking care over the way a change is made, keeping staff fully informed about what is happening, giving them opportunities to contribute their ideas.

It is also clear from these accounts that that alone would not be enough. For the reports clearly confirm the evidence of earlier studies that major changes have a strong political dimension. Battles need to be fought for resources, authority and over the outcome of the change itself. To succeed, several of the managers in this study were putting time and energy into managing their influence, building political support, managing a network of interested parties. These political skills are additional to those associated with the techniques of participative management.

Successful management of complex change projects therefore depends on a new emphasis. Those responsible for driving change need to be able to use skills of political influence, in addition to those of rational problem-solving and participative management; and to move between them as the need arises. And they need to be able to do this in situations where their authority is at best ambiguous, in relation to people in different units, reporting to different line managers:

In order to succeed, you have to meet people, cultivate relationships, be a face.

These interpersonal and political strategies need to be applied externally as well as internally – where the absence of formal authority is likely to be even more marked than when operating within one's own organization.

These skills are not new. They have been part of the management training scene for years, and are not difficult to learn and put into practice. Subsequent chapters of this book will outline what these skills are, and how they have been put into effect by others.

One final puzzle to consider in this chapter is why many of those managing change neglect the use of these skills, given that they are well known, easy to improve and seem to work. Why is the shift in emphasis not widespread? Below is a list of possible explanations which have been suggested to us by project managers when we have put this dilemma to them. Read it, and decide whether any of these factors have been significant in projects you have worked on.

- Project managers tend by nature to focus on the task or the technology, rather than the human aspects.
- Project managers get attracted into the details of the project, the technical bits that seem easier to do, and neglect the more nebulous areas.
- Project managers may have been chosen because of their dynamic style, and that may not include influencing skills.
- Interpersonal skills seem difficult to learn and apply, and it is hard to measure the value of time spent that way (added value v. cost).
- Project managers may be reluctant to consult when the project is still ambiguous.
- Project managers may be reluctant to consult in a hostile environment.
- Senior managers are not aware of problems of driving a project to get it going.
- Rewards are given for tangible results (even if they turn out to be less than was possible).
- The organization 'expects' the technical bits to be dealt with and emphasizes that part of the change management role.
- Overt consultation is not seen as part of the role.
- Sponsor may be unable or unwilling to support broader interaction.
- Project managers may have a desire to avoid confrontation – consultation may divert the project from where powerful champions want it to go.
- There is 'no recognition for being a nice guy'.
- Project managers may raise expectations unrealistically, especially if there is no history of consultation.
- Long-standing differences between people in other departments makes getting agreement on project difficult.

Notepad

- *Which of these obstacles, if any, are likely to apply in your own current project?*
- *What are the implications for how you interpret your role?*
- *How might they affect the outcome of the project?*
- *Are there any others which you would add to the list?*

These factors can be summarized into two different, though overlapping, types. The first six refer primarily to individual factors, while the remainder are primarily organizational.

Individual factors are those which explain the relative lack of attention to the interpersonal aspects of the job by reference to the skills and attitudes of individual project managers: that they are unskilled in these areas, are uneasy with these aspects of the job, find them difficult to learn, and so on. These are clearly factors which the individual may be able to act on directly. They relate to skills which can quite easily be improved, and which can be tried out and developed comparatively easily.

Organizational factors are those that explain the problem by reference to features of wider organizational policy which inhibit or obstruct the use of interpersonal and political skills by project managers. These factors are more difficult to act on, as they may reflect deep-seated beliefs and values in the organization. Changing them will be a longer task.

Personal checkpoints

- Identify the key activities you spend time on during a project.
- Do they match up with the list above, or are there some items missing from either list?
- Work on your roles in the project. What other roles, carried out by others, influence what you have to do?
- Does that identify any skills that you may need to use, but which you do not feel comfortable with?
- How can you go about developing them, or improving your confidence in using them?

4

Who has an interest?

Identifying who needs to be influenced

Change managers need to handle many interest groups, whose support is needed, or whose opposition needs to be overcome. Time is short, so the manager needs a simple technique to identify the key players, to see where to concentrate energy and skill.

Many of the key players identified will be in powerful positions, beyond the influence of any formal authority the project manager may have been given. This makes the skilful use of a variety of influencing strategies critical to effective change management – so guidelines are given as to how this should be approached.

This chapter shows how to identify the interested parties, how to anticipate their reaction, and how to start the process of inflence. The themes are as follows:

> Stakeholders and interest groups.
> Managing in four directions.
> Interpersonal skills for project managers.
> Influencing skills and targets of influence.
> Planning the approach.

Stakeholders and interest groups

These are the people and groups with an interest in the project, and who can affect the outcome. They may be active promoters or supporters of the change, keen to have it succeed. They may be affected by it, though some will not be aware of it. Stakeholders have an interest in the substance and results of the change, and in how the change is managed. They can make a difference to the situation, and project managers need to gain and keep their support.

Making a systematic plan to secure stakeholder support avoids unexpected difficulties. Spending time to anticipate reactions makes the project less vulnerable

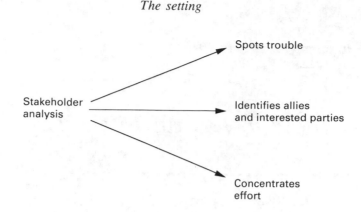

Figure 4.1 How stakeholder analysis can help

to unexpected snags. It helps the project team to spot potential allies and coalitions (Fig. 4.1). It helps the project team to understand the various interested parties in the project:

> If we had carried out a stakeholder analysis during the early stages of the project, and presented it to the team, it would have resolved a tremendous amount of confusion in a single document.

It concentrates time and energy on the most critical groups – those whose attitude will make or break the project – rather than dissipating them over a wide range of interested parties.

The following are therefore key jobs for project management:

- To identify stakeholders, pressure groups, interested parties.
- To assess their interests, and how this will affect what they think and do about the change.
- To manage relations with them – gain their support, minimize opposition and generally create a climate favourable to the change.

Identify stakeholders

In a big change, the manager needs to be aware of the range of interests involved, the number of actors to be dealt with, and the dire consequences of losing their support. They will include external as well as internal interests.

The first step is to prepare a 'stakeholder map' – a diagram showing the main stakeholders likely to need attention. A project manager in a steel company prepared this example. He had been put in charge of a major project to reposition a large piece of production equipment. Two project teams were set up, one from the production division (concerned with the business aspects of the change) and the

---

Highland Express

Following the deregulation of air transport in the early 1980s, many new airlines were established. One of these was Highland Express, which was set up by Howard Fields to offer a new transatlantic service between Scotland and North America. The service proved popular with passengers but, as with any new venture, there were technical and organizational problems. Particular difficulties were experienced with the arrangements for leasing the aircraft required for the service. This led to a lot of adverse publicity, a fall in revenue and unbudgeted costs. Highland Express ceased trading.

Reviewing the experience at a conference a few months after the event, Fields expressed the view that the main reason for the collapse of his business had been that he had not spent enough time keeping his bankers informed of the situation. He had concentrated on the marketing and operational problems; while the banks, upon whom he depended for finance, were left on the sidelines. They became increasingly alarmed about the condition of the business, and eventually withdrew their support. Fields argued that the business was on the point of trading out of the difficulties, but failed because he had ignored, relatively, these key stakeholders.

---

other from the engineering division (who planned and implemented the physical transfer). The project manager, from the engineering division, identified the stakeholders as shown in Fig. 4.2. The map shows not only the large departments most obviously affected by the change, but also some distinct groups within them. These subgroups had different interests and concerns, so it was decided to distinguish them separately at this stage.

Assess their interests

The next step is to assess the interests of the main stakeholders. In the steel company project some of the interests were identified as follows:

- **Sales and marketing.** As short a period of interruption to production as possible.
- **Project team – engineering.** Time to plan the change properly, with as much time as practicable to do it. Treat as human and organization problem, as well as a technical one.
- **Mechanical engineering.** Limit the number of options to be reviewed, given their scarce resources. Treat as a technical problem, which they know how to handle.

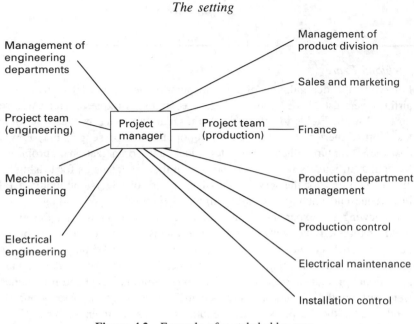

Figure 4.2   Example of a stakeholder map

How to handle them

Having identified the stakeholders and their likely reactions, the next step was to gather ideas on what to do about these interests, and how to ensure their commitment could be gained. The stakeholder map enabled the project manager to identify not only the primary groups involved, but also those at the margin. It gave him a clearer picture of who was involved, so that he was able to plan his approach more confidently.

Another project team, working on an office automation project, also reported their use of the stakeholder map. For them, the particular benefit was that it alerted them to a potential champion for the changes they were planning, who might otherwise have been overlooked. This idea can be put into use by following the steps below.

Preparing a stakeholder map

In the centre of a sheet of paper, write the name of the project you are working on. Then draw other circles around the sheet, each identifying an individual or group whom you regard as having a stake in the project. Place the most significant nearer the centre; others around the edge. Check you have included all relevant interests, including, if appropriate, senior management, colleagues, staff, people in other organizations.

Assessing their interests

For key stakeholders, use a grid like that shown in Table 4.1. Write the key

Table 4.1

Stake-holder	Their goals	Past reactions	Behaviour expected of them	Will change be positive or negative to them?	Likely reactions	Ideas for action

stakeholders down the left-hand side of a sheet, and then summarize your answers to these questions for each stakeholder group:

- What are their priorities, goals, interests?
- How have they behaved in past changes? What clues does that give about possible reaction this time?
- What specific behaviour is expected of them, in relation to the change (e.g. active support on specific tasks, willing to work in a new job)?
- Are they likely to see the change as positive or negative for them? What are they expecting from the project? What is their attitude to it?
- What is their likely reaction? What issues or snags might they raise?

Managing stakeholders

The project manager can then take some practical steps to manage the stakeholders. Questions to work on include the following:

- How can we influence them to support the project?
- What benefits can we offer which they will value?
- How can we sell those benefits?

Note your ideas for action in the last column of the grid.

This assessment and action planning can be done by the project manager alone, or as a planning activity with other members of the project team.

Three other points should be considered.

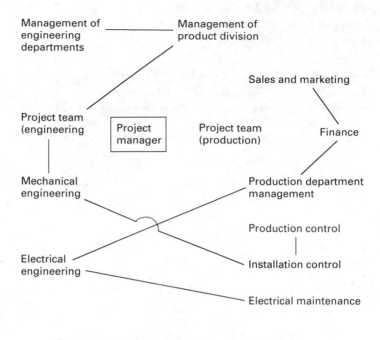

Figure 4.3   Relationships between stakeholders

Relationship maps

What links are there between stakeholders? In the steel company example shown above, the manager also realized that 'natural' links existed, or quickly developed, between some of these interest groups. Some of these are shown in Fig. 4.3. This refinement of the stakeholder map alerted the project manager to actual or potential links that may be relevant to the project:

- How do they presently relate to each other, and will that be affected positively or negatively by the change?
- During the change process, will the reactions of one group of stakeholders affect the attitudes of others? For example, will concessions given to one group affect the expectations of others?
- If two groups have to work together during the project, are they able to do so effectively?

Clearly these ripple effects become increasingly speculative, and it is pointless to anticipate too far. But stakeholders will be talking to each other, seeing what others are getting, and asking what it means for them.

Gatekeepers

Communication between a project manager and stakeholders may be done through another person. This could be the manager of a department whose members have an interest in the change; or the representative on the project team of another group, such as senior management.

Two gatekeepers

A group attempting to introduce a significant change had set up a team consisting of the heads of the main departments affected. It was important to the success of the project that staff in each of the departments were kept up to date with the proposals as they were created, and that their support for the project was secured. It became clear to the person leading the activity that not all the necessary information was being passed on to staff in one area; this was creating bad feeling among the staff there and leading to a negative view of the proposals.

The manager of a project to build a new facility for an industrial chemicals business relied on his boss briefing the Board about progress, and on the business implications of any technical changes which had to be made to the plant specification as the design was worked out. It later became clear that the Board had not been so informed, was unaware of key changes which had been made, and had not realized the difficulties which the project was experiencing.

Both examples show how the process of communication between the project manager and stakeholders can be affected by someone filtering the information flow.

Sleepers

Not all stakeholders will be obvious at the start. Their interests may not be anticipated by project staff, and they themselves may not realize that the project will affect their position. They may still emerge, perhaps at a late stage in the project, and seek to disrupt things if they feel they are threatened.

Should the project manager ignore potential difficulties, only dealing with them if they arise; or is it better to seek them out? One advantage of the latter approach is that the project manager takes the initiative. He or she can choose when and how to raise the issue, rather than have it crop up at an awkward time:

Sleeping directors

A national travel agent introduced a new branch accounting system which, using a networked computer system, automatically transferred reservation details from the retail outlet where the booking was made to head office. This system also enabled a great deal of management information, about the trends in business, and the relative performance of branches, to be provided to management at the centre.

Regional directors of the company had previously been the main source of this information, based on their local knowledge of the branches. They took little interest in the project to install the networked accounting system – until, very late in the project, they realized its implications for their status and security within the company. They then tried, unsuccessfully, to modify the proposed system so as to maintain their control over branch information.

The project was seen from the outset as central to continued efficient operations, and was used to demonstrate the continued viability of the site to groups of stakeholders concerned about security of employment.

The resultant job losses from the project were to be made at a distant site, from amongst a group of employees who did not recognize themselves as stakeholders at the time. They did not yet perceive a threat, but were capable of causing wide disruption once their interests in the proposal were realized.

Timing

The attitudes and actions of stakeholders may change as the project takes shape, and at different phases. For example, in a project to introduce a time-recording system into an insurance company, three principal stakeholders were involved. One had positive attitudes to the change throughout – they were winning in terms of status and rewards at each stage. Another group was negative at first, but became positive later on, while the opposite happened to the third group. For them, initial high expectations disappeared when they became aware of the increased control to which they would be subjected. This can be seen in Fig. 4.4.

The significance of this point is simply to emphasize the dynamic nature of the relationship between the project and the stakeholders. Outside events, as well as the actions of the project manager, affect how interest groups view the project.

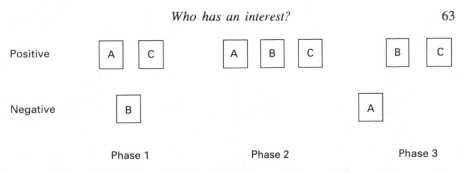

Figure 4.4 How stakeholders' attitudes may change during a project

Sometimes this will bring them round as supporters – at other times the shift will be the other way. The project manager has to be vigilant, not take the current position of a stakeholder as certain, and be alert to external changes which may shift that position.

Notepad

- *When did you last discuss the change with the key stakeholders?*
- *Who are the sleepers and the supporters?*
- *Is there any evidence of gatekeepers interrupting, or enhancing, the flow of information?*
- *What external events might alter the views of particular stakeholders, and how?*

Managing in four directions

It was clear from the accounts of the audio-diarists that the managers adopted different approaches to different groups of stakeholders. This was largely due to the power of the manager relative to the stakeholders, and to what the manager was seeking from the particular target. Managers thus expressed a sense of having to work in several directions at once; analysis of the diaries indicated that this could be more specifically captured by Fig. 4.5.

Managing up

Project managers had to influence the attitudes and actions of senior managers, including Boards of Directors, the heads of their own functions and the heads of other functional areas. They generally needed to exert influence in this direction in the processes of shaping goals, negotiating for adequate resources, or seeking other forms of commitment and support:

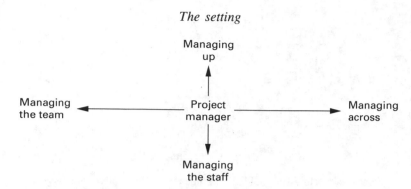

Figure 4.5 Managing in four directions

This is the second time we have been to the management team to pose the problem of how we wish to move forward, and to get them to direct the resources that are required to move us forward. It is, however, worth taking the time up front to get all the members fully supportive of what we are trying to do ... so that by pressure and other means they can try to move (plant X into a more positive attitude).

Often senior managers needed help from project managers to articulate their vision of what the project could do; in other cases, project managers were educating senior managers in what was achievable, and in what realistic expectations might be.

Managing across

Most projects depended on the cooperation of other departments or external organizations, such as subcontractors. Project managers, for example, called on them to provide expert support (as from a computer services function), to advise on functional operations, to provide members for a project team, or to change the way they operated as the changes were brought in. Given different backgrounds and interests, this was often an especially difficult task, not only in ensuring departments knew what was expected of them, but also that they remained committed as changes elsewhere impinged on the departments' resources, and their commitment to the project:

That site is a very important partner in this enterprise, and we have to make sure that their management team understands what we are trying to do, but is also resourced in such a way, and its goals and objectives set in such a way, that they can support this programme. This is additional work, but has to be done before we can even start to get them doing what we need to support our project.

Conflicts and disagreements amongst the key stakeholders needed to be negotiated to a solution, and continuing effort needed to be put into maintaining a sense of ownership in the project.

It was also clear that the project managers needed to build, use and maintain a network of contacts. These were not always directly associated with the problem in hand, but also served the purpose of ensuring that the project managers were kept up to date with changes elsewhere with potential implications for their project.

Managing the team

The audio-diarists needed to gain and keep the motivation and commitment of their project team, whether this was attached to the project part-time or full-time. The temporary nature of such teams, the varied knowledge and interests of their members, and the competing demands on their loyalty, made managing such a group a difficult task. Not only did the meetings of the group itself need to be managed skilfully, so also did the processes and quality of communication between the team and the supporting departments. This was especially true in situations of changing goals and uncertain ownership.

Managing the staff

Finally, project managers needed to ensure the commitment of a wide range of staff, upon whom the success of the change would ultimately depend. Some needed to change their way of working, others were called upon to help the project team design solutions. Others faced the extra pressure of coping with additional work while preparing for the change, and still having to provide a product or service to the customers, using the old system.

All of these activities needed a high level of commitment and motivation to be maintained. This was primarily the responsibility of the manager of their own department – but the project managers were able to affect attitudes and behaviour by the way in which they, and their staff, dealt with the users who would be affected by the planning and implementation of the change.

Interpersonal skills for project managers

Clearly the effective management of a change project requires the exercise of a range of analytical and planning techniques, especially when the project is large,

with many sub-projects having to come together at the right time. These
approaches feature strongly in the early education and training programmes of the
professions from which many project managers are drawn; and they also make up
most of the training available in project management.

The argument of this book is that a new emphasis is needed. To cope with the
introduction of novel changes in a volatile environment, skilled analysis, definition
and control are of course still needed: but they are not sufficient. Change managers
also need to be able to adopt a participative style of management, where this will
encourage a sense of ownership and commitment to the change. And they need to
establish the legitimacy of the change in the eyes of key stakeholders, in a
situation where political considerations are as influential as operational ones. This
combination of skills will enable the change manager to work more effectively in
the uncertain and political environments surrounding major change projects, and to
take the lead in managing the different interests involved.

What does this study suggest are the most essential interpersonal skills which
the project manager needs to use in order to influence others to act in a particular
way?

Communicating

Quite clearly this is a fundamental skill for effective project management. Given
the variety of interests involved, and the rapidly changing environment of the
project, communication failures are never far away. A high degree of sensitivity
and skill in all aspects of the communication process helps information to be
passed around the project in time, and to influence what is being done. This
involves attention to the structured aspects of information flow. Appropriate
communication links and procedures need to be created between the people and
institutions who need to know what is happening.

It also involves skill in written and verbal communication, in face-to-face
situations and in making more formal presentations to large groups. It includes the
critically important activity of listening, of picking up faint signals of events and
people relevant to the change, of generally keeping a finger on the pulse of the
change.

Negotiating

The project manager spends a great deal of time resolving potential conflicts, and
in getting diverse individuals and interest groups to agree on a common approach
to move the project forward. These parties have other interests and priorities, and

it is only by engaging in processes of negotiation that the manager can secure their agreement.

Such negotiations include those that take place in a relatively formal structure, as in discussions with trade unions, suppliers or customers. Equally important are the infinite number of daily occasions on which the project manager is in touch with others, seeking to persuade them to follow a particular course of action.

This will involve him or her in being clear about what is wanted from the other person or group, and in consciously planning what kind of behaviour to use to achieve that result. Whether, for example, to adopt a relatively forthright and assertive approach, to rely on the presentation of reasoned arguments, or to persuade the other side of the benefits of what is proposed.

Team-building

Project managers usually depend on a range of others to help achieve the change – sometimes a rather loosely connected set of individuals, at others a formally established project team. Whatever the particular status of the group, the project manager needs to be able to create a team with energy and enthusiasm, as well as with technical skill.

Particular challenges are posed by the fact that members of such a team are likely to be from different backgrounds, with different interests, and with different degrees of commitment to the change – indeed some may have an interest in the change not happening. They are also a temporary formation, with part of their attention on the current assignment, and part on their future career.

The manager therefore needs to be clear about the different roles ideally present in an effective team, and to shape, as far as possible, the selection process to take that into account. Thereafter the several phases of team development need to be gone through, using established approaches to team or group development.

Involving users and staff

The ability to develop in staff a sense of ownership and commitment to a project, and to the many elements and activities which make it up, is a critical one to have. Many project problems are caused by staff support for the change being taken for granted, with managers unaware of the contribution which those closest to events can make.

The techniques for doing this are well known, including involving those people who will be affected by the change in its planning and implementation, as far as this is practical; the provision of education and training, to ensure that staff are

familiar with the full potential of the new system or procedure; and the reassurance
that support and back-up will be available during the difficult changeover period.
Underlying all of these is a range of skills concerned with consultation, listening
and awareness of the attitudes of those involved.

Influencing skills and targets of influence

The frameworks we have now set out pose a dilemma in how we explore them in
this book. We have identified four targets which project managers will be seeking
to influence; and four broad methods by which that influence can be exercised.

Table 4.2   Methods of influence and targets of influence

	Methods of influence			
Targets of influence	Communicating	Negotiating	Team-building	Involving
Managing up				
Managing across				
Managing the team				
Managing the staff				

These are summarized in Table 4.2. In practice, attempts to influence any of the
targets shown down the left-hand side are likely to draw on any or all of the
methods of influence shown across the top in varying degree, depending on
circumstances. To reflect this reality fully in the chapters which follow would be
very repetitive, so the solution we adopt is as follows.

Each of Chapters 5 to 8 deals with how the project manager can seek to influence
one of the target groups. In doing so, the emphasis is placed on one of the methods
of influence – specifically the one that is likely to be of most use in relation to that
target; but recognizing that others will be drawn upon. For example, the chapter on
managing up will emphasize communication skills – while recognizing that the
manager seeking to influence the Board of Directors may also draw on negotiating,
team-building, or involvement skills to some extent. The arrangement is shown in
Table 4.3.

Planning the approach

Dealing with these issues depends on the manager having an appropriate power
source, and using it effectively. Power itself is only a latent resource. To get things
done it has to be deployed effectively, in a way that people see and respond to.

Table 4.3 Methods of influence and targets of influence – by chapter

| | *Methods of influence* | | | |
Targets of influence	*Communicating*	*Negotiating*	*Team-building*	*Involvement*
Managing up	Chapter 5			
Managing across		Chapter 6		
Managing the team			Chapter 7	
Managing the staff				Chapter 8

We conclude this chapter by outlining a well-established technique for exercising influence, which is common to all the target groups. It enables project managers to make the best use of their position whichever target group is being addressed and whatever method of influence is being used. All of these methods will benefit from time spent planning as indicated below.

The starting point is to focus on the particular event being planned, and to concentrate on specifying very clearly what is to be achieved *by the end of the event.* There will be long-term goals to which this event should contribute, but in planning the exchange, it is essential to concentrate on that event, and on specifying what is to be achieved by the end.

Set the objective. Define as clearly and exactly as possible what is being looked for by the end of the event. Set this out in terms of what the other person or group will do or say, as a result of the meeting. Examples could be as follows:

- 'The team will have agreed to start work on the new project tomorrow, and have agreed a plan of work.'
- 'The manager of department X will have agreed to release a named member of staff to work on the project, and he will be told this later today.'
- 'The manager of department Y will have agreed in principle to stop developing their new system independently, and to set up a meeting next week to look at ways of developing a joint system.'

These are examples of objectives for forthcoming influencing attempts that are clear, unambiguous and which describe intended outcomes that will be observable.

Set measures of success. Express what you hope to achieve from the event more precisely by setting some measurable targets. These can refer both to the end result itself and to the way it is to be arrived at. For the first illustration above these could include the following:

- The team members will themselves set out the timetable.
- At least three proposals for ways of solving the problem will have come from them.
- Two members will have volunteered to work late to finish off the current project while the new one is begun.

- There will be a clear allocation of tasks, with each member's name allocated to one or more of these.
- The agreement will have been reached within two hours.

These give more specific 'sub-objectives' to aim for, and help provide a clear measuring-rod against which to check progress, and what else needs to be done. Not all of them may be achieved, but at least achievement can be compared with targets.

Plan behaviour. Once there is a clear picture of objectives and targets, it becomes easier to decide what to do, and where to concentrate energies. These will depend on the understanding of the situation, power relative to that of the target, and the arguments to be used. Some ideas on how to do this, in relation to each of the target groups, are given in the following chapters.

Personal checkpoints

- Make a stakeholder analysis.
- Check it out with members of the project team.
- Check the assumptions and conclusions with some of the stakeholders themselves.
- Decide who are the key targets of influence.
- Use the method outlined above to decide what you want from those targets (your objectives), and what your measures of success are to be.
- Note some preliminary ideas about how you will try to meet these objectives (your behaviour plan), and then look for additional ideas in the following chapters.

PART II

The skills for managing the process of change

5

Managing up

Communicating with senior management

Project managers cite lack of top management support as one of the most common reasons why projects get into difficulties. That support has to be earned, and argued for, in the face of many competing claims. In some cases, the competition is for resources or other forms of backing which are needed to get the job done – the change agent needs senior support to help solve problems arising in the project, or to show a sense of ownership towards the project. In other cases it may be necessary to get the senior team to give legitimacy to the project. Given the political nature of organizations, a project will suffer if others can challenge or undermine the status or legitimacy of the change: the sponsors of the project may need to 'manage up' to ensure they have a defence against that argument.

The project manager needs to take the lead by putting time and effort into building high-level support – for problem-solving, ownership and legitimizing purposes. As project managers have less formal power than senior managers, they have to become good at using skills which get round this, especially a range of interpersonal ones. As explained in Chapter 4, the whole range may be needed – here we concentrate on communication skills.

The themes of the chapter are as follows:

Creating and selling the vision.
Securing resources.
What are the danger signals?
Communicating skills for project managers.
Ideas for action.

Creating and selling the vision

Projects begin in a loose and unstructured way. Someone has an idea, sees a possibility, observes an opportunity for improvement. Through a process of trying the idea on colleagues, discussing how it might work, lobbying for support, an

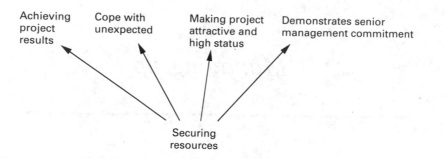

Figure 5.1   Creating and selling the vision

identifiable project comes into being (Fig. 5.1). It is probably still tentative – a feasibility study, a review of the options.

A project manager who is active at this stage can ensure that the project emerges with a clear vision of what the change is for, and has a clear set of objectives. Unless this is done, the later stages of the change will be difficult to handle:

> The size and specification of the project – the tonnages of oils to be made, and the specifications of the products – was not handled well by the commercial functions within the company. It affected results in that when the products eventually emerged from the refinery, we did not have ready customer outlets. Another problem was the decision to develop all our own technology ... this was a mammoth task and would never have been entertained by a major company.

Senior management has other preoccupations, and knows little of the project. They will be unclear about the detailed implications of moving from the broad idea to a realistic plan, and of the problems that will need to be solved on the way through. The project manager will try to engage the attention of senior management in this process.

Visions can easily turn into fantasies – so the project leader needs to ensure that senior managers' expectations are visionary, but also achievable and realistic. The danger of unrealistic expectations seems to be particularly strong in projects involving new technology, where it is easy to underestimate the problems, and to overestimate the benefits:

> A major drawback was that, for a small family company with no experience of implementing a complex project, there was an inadequate allowance for the teething problems to be overcome. They did not appreciate that large, modern process plants are complex in design and layout and need many weeks of familiarization, by skilled operators, before they can be operated efficiently. There seemed to be the idea that once the plant was mechanically

complete, then it was simply a case of pushing a button and product would flow. Of course, in the real world, nothing could be further from the truth.

Senior managers who change the target can wreak havoc on a project. Goals are progressively refined in the early part of a project, through discussion between senior managers and the project manager – who then has to work with the results of that process. Subsequent changes come from two sources:

1. **Novelty** – goals often change simply because of the novelty of the project being undertaken, and an evolutionary process like this makes good sense. Where radical projects are being introduced, the chances are that a great deal of learning takes place as the job progresses – and goals need to be revised in the light of what is discovered about what is, and what is not, possible.

2. **External changes** – A volatile environment will mean that senior managers want to change the direction or goals of the project once it is under way – to take account of new ventures, new opportunities, new threats. Excessive changes, or ones without good reason, cause frustration and disillusion:

> After $2\frac{1}{2}$ years (of failures and changes to plan) the four people who had been trained and enthusiastic at the outset were rapidly becoming demotivated. They were increasingly sceptical of any new suggestion or task.

In any event, the project manager needs to be able to cope with such changes.

The manager also needs to ensure that, as far as possible, they are not made frivolously, or on the basis of poor information reaching senior managers. The wide links of many projects are also a factor here, and one which is easily overlooked by those not aware of the detail. The implications of changes to goals are potentially very wide, and the project manager needs to provide clear signals on this to senior management, not to prevent changes, but to ensure they are made on an informed basis:

> It's vital that the Board realizes that there is a price to be paid for automation, and that it triggers off a whole set of ripples – which cannot then be changed easily.

'Managing up' may include senior managers in other functions or locations, whose support and commitment is needed. While the promoter or champion can see the benefits clearly enough, others may be less convinced, and less inclined to feel a sense of ownership towards the project:

> I then began a round of presentations to plant staffs around Europe, and to our European management team, describing to them the problem, and

Managing change in a health service

The introduction of management budgeting in the National Health Service has placed many new demands on staff at all levels. A manager within the service commented:

> The problem it is designed to alleviate is not voiced or understood by vast numbers of staff in the service. There is a real difficulty in managing a service when we do not have crucial information about costs. But this has not been broadcast sufficiently for professionals to begin suggesting the benefits of a management budgeting system. The service did not identify the problem or the 'felt need', but is trying to implement a solution in isolation. This could open the door to confusion which might have been avoided if the outcome from the system had been clarified initially.

suggesting a way forward. It was in general well received, but it was also clear people were a bit sceptical.

So over the last year my part-time team had done a lot of work with each of their own plant staffs to convince them of the need, and my European functional boss has been doing work with the European management team to convince them. In all, it's taken about fifteen months of part-time work, with the best brains we have available, to try and get our own corporation to move forward. Basically we've been boot-legging for fifteen months across all our European sites to try and put a package together.

Creating a convincing vision of the change is crucial. People expect change to be disruptive – so they need to be convinced the pain will be worth it. The project manager has to work with senior management to create and sell that vision, to give the change a legitimacy which encourages others to support it. Top management setting out convincing reasons for the change and associated turmoil provides a powerful incentive for others to give it their support.

If top management do not see the benefits of selling a major change thoroughly, the project manager may want to persuade them otherwise. Key leaders must feel a need for change, and in turn be able and willing to communicate that to others. If the need for change is not felt, the energy needed to carry it through will not be there and will need to be bought: 'the lower the commitment, the higher the incentives have to be'.

Notepad

- *In what ways are senior managers involved in your project?*

- *How have you worked with them to create a clear vision of the change?*
- *How realistic have they been in their expectations, and what have you tried to do to manage these?*
- *What changes are taking place elsewhere that could affect your project in the next 3–6 months?*
- *Are senior managers aware of the costs of changing targets?*

Securing resources

Big projects need big resources – and the project manager has to secure these from senior management or functional heads (Fig. 5.2).

> The product engineering manager has been championing the project, but no resources have yet been allocated, despite several presentations to senior management. This has resulted in virtually no progress.

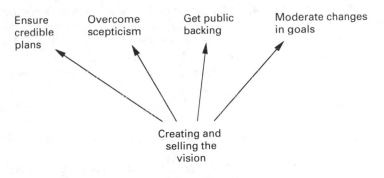

Figure 5.2 Benefits of securing adequate resources

Money and facilities are often less of a problem than staff of the right quality:

> We need people who are good at the travel business, and who can help develop and implement the new systems. Getting people who are good at one of these aspects is OK – but those who are good at both are like gold-dust. And of course the operations side don't want to lose them to the project.

Staff who are put on the project may lack commitment. If they are still attached to a line department, working for the project part-time, they are always likely to be pulled back by their line manager to meet a greater departmental priority:

> The situation in X is no better. In fact it's probably degraded a little bit in the sense that resource in that area has become even tighter, as one of the key individuals is about to transfer inside the company. The Y situation has

gone from bad to worse. One of my key team players there has decided – or his organization has decided – that they have other priorities and he needs to do other work.

And a few months later:

This is the second time we have been to that management team, to pose how we wish to move forward, and to try and get the resources that are required. It is, however, worth taking the time up front to get all members fully supportive of what we are trying to do. Although it takes a bit longer we should, by pressure and by other individuals demonstrating the benefits of the system we are proposing, eventually move them forward.

Maintaining resources is also a problem:

One disappointment (and, I believe, a significant factor in the project) was that just before commissioning, the manager of the pilot plant development team was transferred to another job. He had been promised to me at the project inception, and I had designed him into the working operation.

Securing adequate resources from the top helps the project manager in other ways. It shows in a tangible way that senior management takes the project seriously, and so increases the prestige and authority of those working on it. A well-supported project will be more attractive to people who are asked to work on it. Slack will be available to cope with unexpected difficulties and to use unexpected opportunities.

Notepad

- *How much of your time and effort have you spent getting adequate resources for your project?*
- *Identify a situation where you did secure enough: what did you do to help bring this about?*

What are the danger signals?

There are visible danger signals, which give early warning to the project team of possible trouble with senior management.

Interfering without consultation

Senior managers cannot be expected to know about the details of a project, or its possibilities. This is especially so where new technologies are concerned, with which senior managers are inevitably unfamiliar. They may also be new to the business, perhaps as a result of a change in ownership, or in the distribution of management responsibilities.

The problem this has raised in some projects is that of the professional, experienced manager having to work in a subordinate position to the people who are the paymasters, who have the power, but whose detailed experience in no way approaches that of the experienced professional. For most of the time, senior managers keep out of the way and defer to professional experience, but one of the audio-diarists recalled:

> During the very difficult commissioning period it was apparent that the Managing Director, himself having a technical bias, had formed the view that most of the problems were technical, and that it was necessary to bring in certain consultants to help us. He also allowed another director to recruit a new senior manager from the oil industry. At this time the project was actually technically in good shape, although there were still things to finish off . . . it was becoming apparent that the major problems were now almost entirely commercial, in that markets could not be found for the product.

If they start to get too closely involved, especially without consulting the project manager, difficulties are likely to follow, unless the project manager re-establishes authority.

Not providing support when needed

Senior managers also have other responsibilities, and the current project may not be uppermost in their priorities:

> The development director had significant problems in his own area in the States. Little time could be devoted to interfacing with the UK.

This is highly frustrating for a manager who needs urgent approval for a change in direction, or who needs some high-level support in the fight for resources. A related danger signal would be a senior manager delegating the project to someone more junior or of lower status – especially if they still need to be consulted before major commitments are made.

There are also times when more generalized statements of public support can help the project overcome opposition or inertia:

> The goal of moving into new premises with minimum loss of efficiency was

the fundamental task. This can only be achieved if the workforce shares the goal. To achieve this it was vital that the Chief Executive demonstrated his commitment to change, and I put a lot of effort into persuading him to make a formal presentation to the staff, to explain the plans, and the logic behind them.

If such support is not forthcoming, is this a signal that senior management is either getting out of touch with the project, is losing interest, or is starting to have doubts about it?

Poor communication links

The project needs to have clear, short links to senior management if the change is to meet business expectations, and if senior managers are to be able to keep in touch with progress. An urgent project in a bank suffered from having been set up with an extended link between the project staff and the senior manager on whose support they depended:

> There was plenty of scope for misunderstanding. The Chief Accountant conveyed his understanding of what the legal requirements for the project were to his subordinate. This manager conveyed his understanding of what he thought the Chief Accountant wanted to the business analyst. She conveyed this to the development teams. This structure contributed to the situation where the draft report, which had been agreed with the manager, was not what his boss, the Chief Accountant, wanted.

The danger signal here was the high number of internal linkages, made worse by dependence on an additional external link. To increase the chance of success it would have been necessary to reduce the number of internal links by establishing a more direct line of communication.

Making unfounded promises or commitments

Unrealistic statements or commitments being made should alarm the project manager, for they imply that senior managers have lost touch with the reality of the change project:

> It was apparent to me that X did not communicate the main issues which arose during the project to the Board. For example, when we reviewed the capital requirements, it was some weeks later that I discovered that the rest

of the Board had not been told of our decision to reduce capacity in order to reduce capital cost.

Even when information reaches the top, they may succumb to the well-known traps of ignoring, or discounting, unfavourable information, so frustrating the efforts of the project manager to alert them to impending difficulties and the need for action.

Communicating skills for project managers

Most people are too optimistic about the accuracy of the communication process. Although writing and speaking are relatively easy, achieving understanding is much more difficult. This is true in stable, familiar situations, where people know each other well. In the novel, uncertain and often politically charged atmosphere of major change projects, communication failure threatens every move.

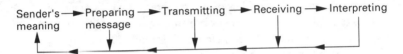

Figure 5.3   Model of the communication process

The communication process is made up of the steps shown in Fig. 5.3.

* **Sender's meaning.** The first step in the communication process is the sender deciding on the message that is to be sent. This is easily taken for granted – but one major source of communication failure is a lack of clarity on the part of the sender about the message they are wishing to convey.
* **Preparing message.** The message needs to be turned into a form suitable for transmission. Choosing the appropriate form of words to use for the audience, deciding how to present them   face to face or in written form. What other techniques should be used in support?
* **Transmitting.** Passing the message to the intended receiver through one or more channels, remembering that communication has not taken place until the intended person has received it. Transmissions will also be taking place that are unintended, through leaks and rumours.
* **Receiving and interpreting.** On receiving the message, the receiver has to attach meaning to it. This will be influenced by the past experience of the receiver, especially with the sender – a message from a previously reliable source will get more attention than one from an unknown correspondent. Filters influence the message that is received. Physical filters limit how much information can be taken in at one time, while psychological filters also affect what is attended to, and how it is interpreted.

The communication process is never, of course, as simple as is implied by this step-by-step process. Several channels are likely to be conveying messages at the same time (such as gestures and mannerisms as well as the intended content of a presentation), and reactions will be affected by events and actions entirely outwith the control of the sender. Above all, the communication process is two-way, with feedback loops passing information back to the sender. The ability to listen is as essential to communication as is the ability to frame and transmit a clear message.

What are the most common barriers to effective communication?

- **Noise.** This is anything that interferes with or distorts the communication process. Too many words, a badly written or confusing paper, the distraction of other events, conflicting messages being received about the same topic.
- **Selective and biased perceptions.** Differences in background and experience mean that people view events and information differently. A person will be reluctant to pay attention to reports on topics which they find tedious, or from a source they regard as unreliable or of low status. Information will be interpreted through the filter of the receiver's own interests and ambitions – an argument that threatens position or status will be viewed much more critically than one that has favourable implications.
- **Language and tone.** The intended meaning of words can easily be misunderstood by those from different backgrounds. A familiar concept to one group may be difficult and obscure to another – impeding communication. Words and phrases which excite one audience will leave another cold – so unless terms are adapted to the audience, the message will be impeded.
- **Lack of feedback.** Receiving a continuous flow of feedback is essential to effective communication – and a lack of it will lead to failure. Listening is as important as speaking – as a way of picking up clues about likely reactions to a proposal, about possible objections and possible solutions. If these are not given, or if the sender of the message does not hear them, they cannot take account of this feedback, risking failure. Listening is a difficult and demanding activity, and one that is essential to good communication.

Ways in which these general principles about the communication process can be applied to the particular situation of 'managing up' in the course of major change projects are outlined in the following section.

Ideas for action

The key strategy for communicating with senior management successfully is to build credibility. It is inherent in the situation that the more junior manager is starting from a position of relatively little power, and is competing with other concerns for the time and attention of senior management. Project managers must therefore aim to give senior managers confidence in their credibility, so that what they say is taken seriously. Some tactics which help achieve this are outlined below.

Create the communication links

Project managers need to review the links they have with the sponsor of the project, the Board, or other senior management. One of the audio-diarists reported:

> My role as adviser to the senior management group means that I am not actually part of that group, and therefore not involved in all issues. It is therefore difficult with something like this to get a hearing for it in that group. Perhaps I need to identify someone within that group to talk the issues through with, and who may then take them forward or help me to take them forward.

The manager of a factory relocation project faced a similar problem:

> One of the most difficult tasks has been the management of the influence of the Group Board. Direct contact between them and the company is limited, and few opportunities exist for the project manager to open communication channels. This makes genuine top management support difficult to secure. The influence of the Board tends to be exerted via the Chief Executive, who may not be the most reliable source of information about attitudes towards the move.

The project manager needs to handle the structure as well as the content of the upward links. The Board will be getting information about the project, even if only in the form of rumours and innuendo. And bad news travels faster than good. So it is in the project manager's interest to ensure that they have accurate, factual information about progress – good and bad.

One project manager who had suffered from poor upward communication links suggested that she could have overcome the problem by:

> targeting the Chief Accountant early in the project as a key person to influence. Regular meetings could have been set up with him, his junior manager and the business analyst. This would have had the benefit of providing a platform for the building of good interpersonal relations, by raising awareness of the differing goals of each party.

It will be easier to win if the sponsor is managed, so that the project has a respected backer, rather than one who is low in status. If necessary, those promoting the change may need to use some initiative to seek out a favourably inclined, *and* respected, member of senior management to provide the link. They must then make doubly sure that that person is attracted by the project, and kept up to date with developments, positive or negative, so that they are always at least as well informed as any other senior manager:

- One made a point of briefing his director fully before each Board meeting during a project, just in case any questions arose. Subsequently he persuaded his sponsor to secure a one-hour spot at every second Board meeting, at which the Board were brought up to date with current information technology issues in the business, and possible future moves.
- A project manager in a local authority identified an elected member who showed an interest in new technology, and invited her to a full briefing on current and proposed systems. This again helped ensure that there was at least one informed opinion being expressed at policy meetings.
- Another recalled that he deliberately solicited the support from a Development Director, in order to influence the rest of senior management.

These examples show project managers actively managing their sponsors. They did not play a passive role, but actively sought out opportunities to build links to the higher levels. In another case, a manager used success in one task to gain power with her boss's boss. Her immediate superior was lukewarm towards the task, but by completing it successfully the project manager showed it could be done. This allowed her to gain visibility and credibility; it also improved her access to the political levels of the organization, to the benefit of later projects. Delivering successfully on something which is valued by senior management is a major tactic in managing up.

Notepad

- *How do senior managers learn about progress on your project?*
- *Is that a good arrangement?*
- *Is the formal communication link satisfactory?*

Get the procedure right

Make sure that the point you are wanting to make is aimed at the right target – that they have the power to meet your request, if you make the case well enough. This includes being sure that you do the following:

- Identify the source of the policy or issue.

- Identify the appropriate manager or group.
- Find out how they operate, what their rules are, what they do and do not like.
- Find out their timetable of meetings, and when items have to be ready for the agenda.

Plan the presentation

This will take time anyway – but if it is to change the views of sceptical senior managers, a lot of work needs to go into the planning:

A great deal of time was wasted earlier, when the choice of the project team was vetoed by the Board, who imposed their own solution. So as I have no direct communication, a more rigorous approach to report-writing must be adopted, to ensure that ideas are communicated with maximum clarity. Although these reports may not necessarily be read by the Group Board, it is more likely that a well-written and well-presented document will be noticed, and less likely that it will be rejected without recourse to the author.

Another project manager drew on past experience to reach a similar conclusion, in preparing a verbal presentation:

Previous presentations had been rejected, because of poor planning, and weak proposals for achieving objectives. The manager was in favour of the concepts, but would not give his support until a detailed plan was presented. To manage upwards in this company, the presenter must anticipate all questions, and present the data in a logical and concise manner. So the new presentation contained both Gantt and Pert charts for the first time. It was accepted.

A project leader for a radical information system in a bank depended on top management support against attacks from another service department. He and his team made presentations about the intended system to senior managers, which appeared to work:

Each demonstration was carefully planned and rehearsed. Credibility was also gained by using the external consultant's experience, where he had introduced similar projects in major high street banks.
The system was demonstrated to a key manager, who was also the Deputy Chairman of one of the businesses. He was impressed by what he saw, the ease of use, and immediately ordered a personal computer for his own use. This information was made known to all concerned, and soon even those who had sworn never to have a personal computer were ordering one too.

Planning also includes thinking through exactly what should be achieved by the end of a presentation, whether written or face to face. That should be expressed in terms of specific results, such as, 'By the end of the meeting, the manager of European distribution will have agreed to release one member of staff to the project for two weeks.'

Then think out how best to handle these practices which will increase the chance of success:

- **Manner of presentation.** Think out who will receive the proposal, or be at the meeting to discuss it. Consider what their interests are, and how they are likely to view the proposal. What might allay their fears, enhance their commitment? Use the right language – think of the perspective from which the audience will view it. This will probably mean phrasing recommendations in the language of finance or business, rather than of technology or human relations.
- **Facts and data in support.** Successful attempts to influence senior managers are backed up by convincing evidence. Find out how others have dealt with similar changes and give examples of how what is proposed has worked elsewhere. Find out who you know there, and arrange to learn from their experiences. Decide on the best arguments, evidence, examples that senior managers will be able to identify with.
- **Supporting documentation.** Decide what material to send out before a meeting, and how it should be prepared. It has a better chance of success if it shows knowledge of current policy relevant to the matter, and is presented concisely and reasonably, in clear terms, without technical jargon.
- **Present a complete plan.** If possible, present a worked-through solution, not one that evidently needs further work. The key is to make their decision easy, and the more confidence you can give them, by showing the proposal has been thought out, the more likely it is that senior managers will approve.

Impression management

As well as ensuring a convincing presentation goes to senior managers, the project manager can enhance its chances of success by tactics which create a receptive attitude amongst senior management. These include the following:

- **Show the support of others.** Attempts to influence senior managers are more likely to succeed if the proposal is backed by other groups. The project manager therefore needs to prime key people to write or speak in support of the project. They could be other line departments, or staff groups such as personnel or finance. Persuading them to act on behalf of the project will in itself be an exercise in influence.

- **Build your image.** People pay more attention to information from a known, respected source, so you can strengthen the impact of your presentation by doing things which enhance senior management's impression of you. Dress and act like them; make sure the preparations for your meeting are done well; prepare written reports in a way that adds weight and authority to the case you are making.
- **Create opportunities.** Do not always wait to be asked to present ideas to senior managers. Take the initiative by looking for opportunities where you can get your views across – forthcoming meetings, presentations, seminars. Take or create opportunities to meet as many as possible informally before a meeting, to sense their reaction, and to get clues about areas of concern or opposition.
- **Timing.** There are always competing pressures on senior management time. Think carefully about when to push a thing, and when to hold back. What events or changes are imminent that will make senior people more receptive to what you propose? Or do you have to act very quickly now, to seize the best chance you will have for months?
- **Persistence and repetition.** Senior management may not pay attention straight away, and the project manager needs to be prepared to persist with their argument. This can be highly discouraging, and adds to the vulnerability of the role. A project manager wanting senior management attention needs to remain visible and prominent:

> It's the same as happens to some product design in its early days. An individual or a group of individuals need to go out on a limb with an idea, and be able to articulate that idea to a wider audience before they can get any interest and therefore any support and investment to go forward.

Personal checkpoints

- Make a list of the key ways in which senior management could act to help the project forward.
- Identify how the project is linked to senior levels of the organization. Note some examples showing when this has worked well, and some when it has caused problems.
- Identify how the link itself could be improved, and whose support you want to get.
- Review the stages of the communication process outlined above, and identify possible pitfalls at each stage. Plan how to handle them.
- Review the causes of communication failure outlined earlier, and note down

any that seem likely to arise in your project. Use the ideas above as a starting point for planning how to avoid them.

- Select one idea from those above, make a detailed plan to use it, and then try it out.

6

Managing across

Negotiating with colleagues

Project managers usually depend on people in several departments or functions being willing to put energy into the project. They engage in negotiations with them to establish a shared sense of ownership in the change, reflected tangibly in the release of adequate resources. They want the separate areas to work together in a consistent manner, both in planning the change and when it is in regular operation.

The areas concerned probably report to a different senior manager and have their own priorities and interests. They may be indifferent to the project or strongly opposed to it, especially if it conflicts with personal ambitions. They may also be under pressure from other changes taking place in the business – and can only cope with so much. Project managers need to spend time and effort anticipating what they need from other areas, and securing their ownership and support. They may also need to persuade other departments of the legitimacy of the change, in competition with other interests. They need to work out where to start, to whom to talk, which groups to involve.

This will involve the use of negotiating skills. Often thought of as a relatively formal bargaining activity, negotiating is a common feature of the change management process. It occurs wherever two or more parties have limited resources, and when progress on the project depends on one of the parties gaining some from the other – such as staff, time, space or any of the other resources needed for the project.

The themes are as follows:

Ensuring consistent planning and implementation.
Creating a sense of ownership.
What are the danger signals?
Negotiating skills for project managers.
Ideas for action.

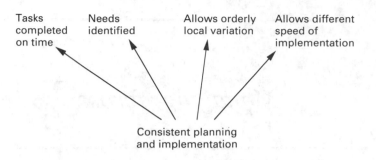

Figure 6.1 Benefits of consistent planning and implementation

Ensuring consistent planning and implementation

The problem of coordination between functions is as old as organizations. The more outside links that are part of a project, the more problems they will create, and the more 'managing across' the project manager will need to do. Small projects present few problems, as most of what is needed lies within the control of the manager responsible. The larger the task, the more likely it is that success will depend on integrating the work of others, especially if goals and links are changing (Fig. 6.1).

A failure:

The main reasons for the failure of the project was the lack of market development activities. Another was the inexperience of us all in getting to know the technology. The failure to sustain a good relationship with a key supplier was a critical factor, as was the delay caused by the dismissal of a subcontractor.

A success:

As the project unfolded, the company really grew into three distinct areas – one arranging finance for the development, a second concerned with introducing the technology and making sure it worked, while a third carried responsibility for continuing operations. I don't believe that any of this could have happened without each of these three functions being successful in its own element of the business. Close involvement with the supplier also helped – their skill gave us the confidence to go ahead, and to keep going.

In both cases, progress depended on work being done in separate units. In the first example, the lack of consistent progress by these departments caused major problems for the project.

Consistency does not have to mean complete uniformity. Project managers have sometimes found it possible, even desirable, to balance a search for consistency with scope for local adaptation – to meet local conditions, to maintain staff commitment and interest, or simply to prevent a problem area delaying the whole project. A project to develop a common system amongst the European plants of an electronics company ran into difficulties, as each was at a different stage of development. In the words of the project manager:

> We have seven sites, each with their own characteristics and problems, and each at different stages of development. We have to make sure that each is positioned in terms of resources, energy and commitment to support an integrated programme. Now we have a business that is both complex and diverse; so we have adopted an approach that generates a common level of understanding about what needs to be done, but which then allows each area to specify their unique requirements within this overall framework. It also allows each individual location to move at their own pace, as long as they don't exceed a maximum that we all agree.

Similar flexibility, within a broadly consistent framework for implementation, was reported from a local authority, where some departments displayed resistance and uncertainty:

> There were, however, some cases of resistance to change and instances of protectionism. This had an effect on how, when and where the project should progress. We implemented in the areas where we had total support so that when we reached the areas where we were expecting opposition, we had proved our point and we were able to display examples of our success.

The project manager will be balancing the needs of different departments. Those that are keen to press ahead may need to be slowed down, while those that need to move more slowly are given more time. But the interests of the latter cannot be protected so well that the enthusiasm of the former is lost.

There will be limits on the scope for local variation. Where all units must at some stage be part of a new system, the project manager must exercise skills other than patience. That will be easier if credibility with top management has already been built up. This dilemma, of how long one can allow an area to fall behind the project as a whole, was experienced by one of the audio-diarists:

> If I'm unable in January to persuade that team to participate fully in the programme, I may have to take the fairly drastic step of reconvening the senior management team, and possibly recommend excluding that business unit from the programme.

The project manager also depends on separate functions providing accurate information about current operations and likely future needs – otherwise the most basic aspects of the project can be incorrectly designed. This takes time, and commitment. Without that, other departments will not respond, or will do so in an unhelpful way.

Notepad

- *Are any imbalances arising between the rate of progress in separate parts of the project?*
- *How serious is that likely to be?*
- *Why do you think that is?*

Creating a sense of ownership

People need to 'own' a problem before they will be willing to invest time and effort to making a change work. Some functions or departments who need to be involved in the work will have no difficulties in demonstrating this, but others will feel the project is distracting them from their more urgent priorities. The project manager must build a sense of ownership amongst other departments towards the project, so that it is not seen as someone else's problem (Fig. 6.2).

The most tangible benefit of doing so is the willingness of other units to release resources. They are likely to be the main source of staff for a project – and the project manager will usually experience difficulty getting enough of the right people released. The pace of change makes this more difficult:

> The plant at Z is currently going through a major increase in demand for its products and this is having to be met without increasing cost, in particular manpower, to a degree that one might have done in the past. Innovation is therefore required. Innovation takes energy, and the Z management team are engaged in trying to meet this market demand and at the same time support my programme. This puts a lot of stress on the system.

Change usually depends on other units being willing to alter the way they work.

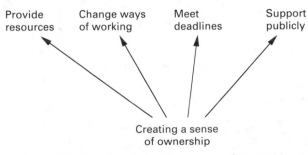

Figure 6.2   Benefits of creating a sense of ownership

The manager of a group whose project involved designing new electronic devices recalled that this depended on other groups being willing to change the way they did their part of the task. Unfortunately:

> other product groups were not prepared to alter their design methods at that particular time, to allow their devices to be fitted easily into our system. This made it impossible for us to offer the full range of possibilities to the customer.

The manager of a group planning an information system in a bank faced a similar problem, which he overcame by sending strong signals to establish the legitimacy of the project in the eyes of those who were expressing reluctance to support it:

> The next issue to be considered was that of the links between the MIS development group and the other service departments. Once the system was implemented, the Operations Department would assume responsibility for operating it on a weekly and monthly basis. Initially they were reluctant to change any of their current procedures, citing lack of resource as a major constraint. When it was made clear that the original sponsor of the project was the Head of Technology, their attitude changed. They started to listen to what was being proposed, and soon became very enthusiastic when they realized this was an exciting new challenge, and that it was wanted by senior people in the bank.

Another of the audio-diarists consciously kept in touch with developments elsewhere in his organization, as an insurance policy against unexpected developments that could be of interest to his own objectives:

> We are keen on developing a comprehensive client record system. We are therefore interested in the office automation projects that are going on in the council, and may wish to pursue those. We also want to look at the social service client record system again to see if that could be any use to us. Basically we need to be kept better informed as to what the council is doing, appreciating that they are changing their strategy. Gives us time to think about it, and they are thinking about it at the same time.

The project manager also expects other departments to meet deadlines set, come up with ideas to overcome difficulties and generally to support the project publicly. This will only happen if the staff in the respective functions feel a sense of ownership and responsibility towards the change.

Notepad

- *Which other departments or functions does the project depend on?*
- *For each of these, how committed do you feel they are to the change?*
- *How has their respective degree of commitment affected the change so far?*

What are the danger signals?

When a change involves extensive work with other departments, danger signals such as those set out below warn the manager of impending problems.

Physical distance

It was clear from the audio-diarists that the greater the physical distance between the departments that needed to work together on a project, the more difficult they became to manage – even with modern technology. Responsibilities are harder to tie down and even harder to monitor – making it difficult for staff in other locations to know what is expected.

This is a problem if they are in the same building – but it is an even more acute danger if they are physically distant, which is now often the case:

> The project manager was also successful at managing across the relevant departments, even with wide geographical separation, development being in Birmingham and operations in Glasgow. He achieved shared ownership after overcoming initial resistance. They had many other systems, all important, and did not want to change priorities.

The greater a project depends on consistent action by separately managed functions, and the more distant these are, the more effort the project manager needs to put into getting their informed cooperation.

Giving low priority to the project

The departments the project manager needs to work with have their own priorities and resource constraints. In a dynamic business all functions are likely to be under pressure. They have their own current targets to meet, so the project manager seeking time or other resources for a development activity finds it extremely difficult to get people to focus on the important rather than the urgent.

Signs of other things taking precedence include the persistent over-running of deadlines; staff not attending meetings; relatively junior or low status staff being sent to meetings, when more senior people are required; excuses rather than results being delivered.

Recalling previous failures

Past experience also affects attitudes to a current project, and a department reluctant to take part is likely to recall earlier difficulties, perhaps with embellishments. The promoter of a major project in a multinational experienced this:

> They were a little sceptical and wary of whether it was actually going to enhance our processes. Major pan-European redesign work had been attempted in the past and had failed miserably. The solutions had not been appropriate and had not been accepted by the divisions. Europe-wide programmes therefore had a bad name.
>
> One area was not necessarily outwardly hostile to the idea but they felt there was one computer system in operation already, and they don't see the benefit from that system. They have been sending in masses of information and getting back masses of paper – but nothing that really helps them to do the job. So they are not very keen on the new idea.

And similarly:

> There are so many changes taking place, they are more or less numb, and this is simply another change which they are just going to have to take on board. The result is that they are somewhat passive and neutral, and when I ask what their requirements might be, the response is usually 'you tell me'.

On the other hand, he also noted that:

> others are very keen and keep phoning me up with suggestions, asking me to keep them in touch with developments, which is, of course, perhaps a little puzzling ... you've got to be careful about the politics – the political situations are liable to get out of hand.

Political obstacles being raised

Politics may also be involved – as in the company where a development team in one European country working on product A of the corporate plan found their progress obstructed by the manager of another business unit. The objections had no operational basis, which led the manager of the development team to conclude that political factors were at work. It transpired that the other manager favoured the development of product B, and that he had ambitions to take over the development unit and integrate it on the site he controlled directly.

Negotiating skills for project managers

A key point for project managers negotiating with another department or unit to remember is that they will probably need to work with them again. So it is important to conduct the negotiations in a way that helps to build and maintain good long-term relationships. The following tactics, based on studies of effective negotiators, will help project managers develop their skills in this area.

Preparation

As in all attempts to influence the behaviour of other people, preparation pays off in negotiating. Refer back to the section in Chapter 4 on 'Planning the approach', and use that as a guideline in your preparations. Specifically, you will need to identify the objectives you are hoping to achieve by the end of the negotiation, what standards or targets you are hoping to achieve, and what you will do in order to reach those targets. Write down your objectives, targets and behaviour plans, try them out with your colleagues, perhaps rehearse some of the more important arguments you want to use. Then read the rest of this section, which gives some ideas on negotiating practice.

Label your behaviour

Skilled negotiators are clear communicators, and one technique they use is to signal that they are about to suggest a solution, or to ask a question. It has the effect of catching the attention of the whole group, and putting pressure on the person to whom the signal has been directed. Without the clear labelling, the target may be able to avoid responding – but the label makes their position more visible to everyone present.

Test and summarize

A very useful technique, especially in a long negotiation, is to test that both sides fully understand what is being proposed, and have a common understanding of the stage the negotiations have reached. This helps to clarify key points, and also helps to create mutual trust. It shows that although you may not accept the other side's point, you have listened to it sufficiently well to be able to summarize the argument. Above all, the practice of testing and summarizing helps to ensure that when an agreement is reached, it is not undermined by misunderstandings amongst the parties about what was being agreed.

Do not dilute a good argument

It may seem that the more individual arguments you can bring out in support of a case, the more persuasive the case becomes. This is not the case – skilled negotiators tend to use fewer, but stronger arguments, rather than a lot of weak ones, to support a position.

A weak argument does not add to a strong one – it dilutes and weakens it. The reason is that a skilled opponent will spot the weakest in a series of points being made – and attack it hard. This tends to put the other side on the defensive very quickly, and to undermine the credibility of their case as a whole.

Use questions to persuade

The negotiator is obviously keen to get his or her point of view over to the other side, and a common fault is to stress, repeat or emphasize an argument that is not being accepted. Repeatedly telling a person something, which they are clearly unwilling to accept, is unlikely to change their view – if anything, it will reinforce their opposition.

A better approach is to ask the other side questions – carefully designed to let them realize the strength of your case. Good negotiators ask a lot of questions, which gradually reveal the legitimacy of their point. Allowing the other side to think about the issue in a particular way is more likely to reduce their opposition, and thus secure their agreement. Trying to force acceptance on them is unlikely to work.

Use questions to control

Asking questions gives the questioner more control over the conversation. The other side is forced to respond to what is being asked, rather than leading with points which they wanted to make. It also gives the questioner more thinking time – while the other is responding to the question, the questioner can be planning his or her next move.

Skilled use of a question also allows the negotiator to avoid disagreeing directly with the other side's proposal. So instead of saying 'that wouldn't work here', the skilled negotiator would say something like 'Could you please tell me how that might work here?' If the question allows the other side to see the weakness of their idea, the point is won: if they can respond convincingly, the questioner is no worse off, as their disagreement would have been countered anyway.

Plan your questions

Since questions play such an important part in negotiations, prepare, and write down before the negotiations, a list of questions you are likely to want to use. They will not only help you to persuade and control – they will also come in useful if you get into difficulty, and want to take the pressure off. Asking a question, to which they have to think up a reply, gives you time to think.

Ideas for action

The key strategy in managing across is to negotiate with a range of outside interests, so as to integrate their interests with those of the project. The project manager has to ensure that these other interests give what is needed to the project, mainly by negotiating with them about the benefits that can be offered in return. Some tactics and practices which will help are set out below.

Find out whose commitment you need

Work out, by using the stakeholder analysis in Chapter 4, who will have an interest in the project, and whose support will be needed for a successful conclusion. Then set out exactly what it is that is wanted from them, during and after the project. Until it is clear what they are expected to provide – staff, premises, changes in the way they work, political support, and so on, little will happen. Establishing such targets – how much? when? for how long? – is the first step in the process of influence.

The interests of the stakeholders themselves also need to be understood and taken into account as far as is practicable. The change needs to be viewed from their point of view. While to the project manager the changes proposed will look positive and exciting, others may see them as threatening, time-consuming and foolish.

Priorities and expectations should be presented in a way that seems reasonable to them. Make your approaches in a way that is sensitive to this, and which recognizes the need to earn their willing cooperation. People may follow instructions, but this may not be the most productive approach in the long run.

Prepare to discuss not only the preferred solution, but also what would be acceptable as a fall-back position. Decide the arguments you will use, and try to anticipate their likely reaction. One way of anticipating the reactions of interested parties is to ask persistently, before making a move, 'who will that affect, and who am I likely to upset next?'

What benefits can be offered?

In return for the commitments sought from other departments, the project manager needs to consider what rewards and incentives can be offered in return. What benefits can be offered that they will value? For example, giving a group a particular task may help their promotion chances, give them visibility amongst senior managers, or provide them with opportunities to build a network of contacts.

The project manager may win support by providing a department with resources or assistance that they need for other aspects of their work. One of the audio-diarists gave an example of this, when he recalled persuading a unit to give him systems support, by arranging for the unit to be given extra staff in another area. Another who wanted a department to change priorities in favour of his project recalled:

> The tactic used was to offer task-related help, in this case with problems they were experiencing with other MIS systems. In return the project team received the desired commitment to the project. This task was made easier by the existing good working relationships already built up.

Notepad

Which of the following types of benefit could you try offering to one of the groups you want to influence?

- *Promotion or better career prospects.*
- *Career visibility.*
- *Networking in high status groups or places.*
- *Other valued staff resources.*
- *Task support in another area of work*

Have you tried taking such an approach?
How well did it work, and why?

Involve other functions in shaping the project

A critical stage in project management is that at which the broad idea is turned into a tangible target. If other functions, even external organizations, can be involved in this phase, they are more likely to support the project later. The following is a good example of this idea being put into practice:

> Very soon after the project was established, the manager called for a one-week brainstorming team-building session. All managers of the various [world-wide] groups reporting to the Vice-President participated, including representatives from the European Business group. As a result of this meeting, relationships were established and objectives agreed. The meeting developed overall objectives for the project, which translated into specific tasks for our group. I saw it as a major benefit for the participants, and helped gain the commitment of the functional areas to become involved in these state-of-the-art developments.

Explore how fully stakeholders, internal and external, can take part in design, especially if they are to be direct users of the system, and likely to be working on it after the change. This is a benefit which most users value, and greatly helps the integration of the project:

> One of the key factors for success was having the users participate in the project from the start. The project team had ensured that users had participated throughout, reckoning that once committed to the project, they would want it to succeed. For example, we developed a prototype of the system very early and showed it to some of the key users, who were asked:
> 'Is this the information and type of system you envisaged? If not, could you please tell us why, and what you would like?'
> The users were greatly encouraged by what they saw, and their manager immediately agreed to have more discussions with his counterparts in other regions, which would result in a reasonably well-defined requirement for the new system. The project was born.

Consider whether clients of the project could be involved in design, and placed in key positions on the project team. Listen to the ideas and comments of the interest groups. They probably have a point, even if they seem misguided or ill-informed. And even if the point itself is no use, having it aired and discussed can keep a group or department on board:

It was noted in my appraisal last year that I should pay more attention to 'bringing people along with me'. The project reinforced this. Instead of dismissing ideas as irrelevant at the outset, I accepted these and so gained the support of the proposers. In assessing the interests of stakeholders, it became evident that I needed their support. The project proved to me that bringing people along until we all shared the same view was essential to gaining commitment and enthusiasm.

Another project manager had used the close involvement of staff to overcome the dilemma of a national system requiring local commitment:

we involved local supervising management in planning how to put the overall scheme into their area. This introduced and involved them at an early and critical stage in the project, and we were able to benefit from their local knowledge and experience.

Making a conscious effort to allow as much local variation in design as possible gave valued benefits. Decide which elements in a project *must* be consistently applied – and which parts can be locally designed.

Starting well does not in itself guarantee success. This was illustrated by some later comments about the successful team-building work described above. The initial euphoria gradually dissipated:

While kicking-off the change in an ideal fashion, the lack of similar follow-on meetings contributed to the political moves, and to concerns over apparent shifts of power. If meetings had been held more regularly, some of the problems could have been highlighted and addressed in a more constructive and productive manner.

Build good relationships

It is vital that good relations are built and maintained throughout the project with the departments whose help is needed. Apart from the project-centred meetings and negotiations, people in other areas value being kept up to date more generally with what is going on in the project. Tell them what is happening elsewhere. Do they have other problems that the project manager can help them with? Always be on the look-out for ways of building up credit with managers or staff in those departments, making it more likely that they will give support when it is needed.

Ensure that there are formal communication links with clients or other interested parties, otherwise there is a danger that information is only passed on haphazardly. It may be wise, for example, to ensure that regular communications to those concerned are done through the steering committee, as well as through more informal, short-term, devices.

Communicating with subcontractors

A company engaged a subcontractor on a project, and it quickly became clear to the company's project manager that the subcontractor was not up to the job. The subcontractor's site manager, in fear of his job through the poor progress of the project, failed to act as a communication link between the project manager and the senior management of the subcontractor. Realizing this, the project manager had to create his own direct link, bypassing the site manager.

Functions which are not directly involved in, or benefiting from, the project are likely to take longer to build up enthusiasm for it than those with most to gain. If project managers press too hard for a quick result, they run the risk of alienating those whose support they need. A sense of ownership takes time to develop, and the project manager thus needs to know when to be ready to allow the work to slow down for a period. This effort to build the relationship, by recognizing the other department's difficulty, will usually pay dividends later:

> You need patience and tolerance – but also knowing when to act quickly, and when to stand back. You have to learn to live through a lot of slow patches to get to a solution.

The relationship can also be strengthened by testing ideas early. Informal discussions are a vital part of this – building a network of links, and maintaining that network, is a vital source of 'soft' information. By actively seeking ideas from other departments, the manager can try out new ideas or potential proposals and gauge possible reaction. This gives clues about whether it is worth working along a particular direction, or whether it would be a waste of effort.

Personal checkpoints

- Ensure you have a stakeholder map showing all the interested parties, with the key ones identified.
- Check that thought has been given to their interests, and to ways of keeping them up to date with the project.

- Allow time for a sense of ownership in the project to develop – other groups may take longer to see its value than those most directly involved.
- Check that the priorities and objectives set take reasonable account of stakeholder interests, or that there are good reasons for not doing so.
- Create appropriate rewards and penalties to encourage support, and to discourage opposition.

7

Managing the team

Building an effective project team

Project managers need help – usually obtained by creating a group of people to work with them during the change. Where the project is narrowly focused, the members are likely to be from similar backgrounds, and probably fit the normal pattern of working relations. Where the changes are novel, uncertain and relatively open-ended, success depends on bringing a deliberately diverse group of people together, and working to bring them into a committed and enthusiastic team. That puts heavy demands on project managers' team-building skills. The themes of this chapter are as follows:

> Providing a focus for the project.
> Driving the project.
> Making the most of diversity.
> What are the danger signals?
> Team-building skills for project managers.
> Ideas for action.

Providing a focus for the project

Projects are not always clearly established as distinct tasks – sometimes they are hard to identify amongst all the normal, regular activities of the organization. In such cases, they run the risk of being nobody's problem, and therefore of failure. One of the prime functions of a project team is simply that such a team gives visibility and recognition to the task, by attaching some names to it.

The 'project team' implies a more defined and identified group of people than is often the case. We need to clarify whom this chapter is about. We also recognize that not all project managers have a project team – some have to do it all themselves.

The overall direction of large, long-term projects is usually by a steering group.

A team provides focus

A project to develop a new process had come into being in an electronics company. It was crucial to the company's position in the market, was novel and controversial. Yet it took a long time to get started, and progress was slow. Local management then realized that other parts of the organization were starting to take an interest in the project, and that they would be vulnerable if things did not speed up. An engineer with the company commented:

> When this fact was realized, a group was formed to monitor the progress and take the necessary action to ensure its smooth passage. A project team should have been formed much earlier, rather than when problems arose.

This is typically made up of senior managers, often with some external or non-executive advice available as well. It meets relatively infrequently, monitors progress and serves as a link between the details of the project and the wider activities of the enterprise. The project manager will be a member of this group, and it is one of the main mechanisms of 'managing up'. But the manager working on the detail of the change is normally in the position of reporting to the steering group, rather than leading it or of having much say in how it does its work. Although the ideas in this chapter will be relevant to that group, it is not the main focus.

In shaping the change, the project manager will spend time with many people affected by the project. He or she calls on them for advice and guidance, makes presentations to them, listens to their views and generally calls on their skill and knowledge to move the project forward. But the project is not a major element in their work, and their contact with project management may be quite brief. They are the focus of the next chapter, not of this one.

The focus here is the small group of people who work with the project manager on a relatively continuous basis, for the duration of the change. The project is expected to be an identifiable part of their job:

> The project team consisted of a process engineer from each section, a product engineer and a team leader. The team was set the objective of organizing the manufacturing flow for the trial silicon. Each member knew what tasks they had to perform as they were directly related to their normal job function.

Another recalled:

I was assigned as leader of this project, so my role was to lead a team of management services officers [to work through the change].

A few project managers are able to build a team specifically to work on this project: most make do with part of their time, in competition with other work. Sometimes the manager selects the team – others have little choice, and have to work with those who are there.

There may be other teams working on other change projects, or on other aspects of the same project. Unless carefully managed, this causes irritation or confusion amongst other groups or staff (from whom information may be sought), and the teams may end up competing for territory. Alternatively, an issue may slip because each thought the other was dealing with it.

If there is any uncertainty about whether people see themselves as part of the project team, or about the relationship between the team and the steering group, or between teams working on different change projects, this needs early attention.

Driving the project

Project teams are created to drive the project forward, to generate ideas and generally to handle the range of issues that will need to be dealt with, during the project, and in some cases, after it (Fig. 7.1).

Figure 7.1   Benefits of an effective team

Some project teams are created to deal with a relatively structured part of the overall task. For example, senior management in a semiconductor business decided to enter a new market, and created a new division for the purpose. Part of the project was to be handled by the company's Scottish plant, and a development team was created there to develop expertise in the new tools, and to support a European design network by providing a service in the area of expertise the Scottish team would develop. The local manager arranged for four of his engineers to participate in the project. He was

excited about the possibility of getting his team involved in this state-of-the-art design development. The strategy proposed would make the local group stronger, enhance their skills and result in even more challenging and rewarding tasks for the engineers. The team members had each been chosen for their ability to assimilate the skills quickly. Each agreed enthusiastically to participate.

In other cases, the team is intended to perform a range of tasks, but within a general direction that is already decided. For example, the project manager of the company which had decided to create a new refinery built a team to look after the detailed design and construction of the plant:

> I personally started to recruit the staff required for the refinery, beginning with the current refinery manager who was to be my main assistant for the commissioning period. We also recruited the shift supervisors, operatives and other specialists who would be required. An important feature of the project was to weld the staff together as a team, and to ensure that they all had adequate training in order to run the refinery efficiently and safely. As well as the seasoned operatives, we decided we would take on younger, graduate-type employees who had little experience but lots of energy and enthusiasm. This blend within a shift seemed to work well.

He saw the team-building aspect as a major part of his role:

> Perhaps the main demand on my skill and competence lay in my managerial role that I had to lead a small professional team. I needed to motivate them through the design, procurement and erection stages, and then also in the difficult commissioning stage.
>
> I adopted a role as a working manager, leading from the front, frequently donning overalls and working with the men on the refinery in whatever mundane jobs they were doing. I also tried to maintain an overview of events.

In another example, the project was still at the conceptual stage. The man who had set the idea moving realized the benefits of deliberately bringing the power of a team to bear on his novel and creative project, and accordingly:

> We gathered a group of people together from each location who understood what order-processing was about, and who also had a vision of what it could be like in the future. We had two five-day meetings, and came up with the bare bones of a proposal.

Having run into some difficulties:

> Again the part-time team set to work, pulling together their thoughts and

their ideas, and drafting it into a document. It took about three months, and [after further work] we eventually managed to capture the interest, imagination and energy of a senior group, and very clearly they were going to try and find a way, even though we have no formal budget, to make a European scheduling programme happen.

Notepad

- *Review the 'team' that is helping you to manage the change.*
- *How clearly and formally has it been set up?*
- *How clearly have its responsibilities and powers been defined – and how widely publicized?*
- *Are the members full-time or part-time?*
- *Which of the three benefits cited above do you want most help on from the team? What else do you want from them?*

Making the most of diversity

In all the examples above, the managers referred to the diversity of the project team. They took care to bring together a variety of skills and experience, which would contribute in different ways to the overall task.

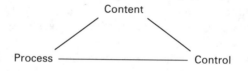

Does the team have skills for them all?

Figure 7.2   The three agendas of change

One perspective on this diversity is to remember that a well-balanced team needs to have members who, as a group, can deal with the three agendas of change set in Fig. 1.1 and reproduced in Fig. 7.2.

To deal with the *content agenda*, the requirements would include the following:

- expertise – in payment systems, planning systems, new technology or whatever it is that the project concerns.
- policy awareness – someone able to link the work on the project to the wider policies and strategies of the organization.
- operating knowledge – current, accurate knowledge of how the relevant part of the enterprise works.

To deal with the *process agenda*, the requirements could include the following:

- team-building skill – able to help the disparate members of the team learn to work together.
- awareness of process – those who are conscious that the way things are done matters as much as what is done; both within the team itself, and in its relations with others.
- time and commitment – willingness and ability to give the time needed to be an effective team member – and that their boss accepts this.

Finally, to cope with the *control agenda*, it helps to have the following:

- helicopter view – someone able to see the broader picture, within which the project needs to fit.
- time-keeper – not necessarily in the literal sense, but simply someone aware of how the project is progressing, and how that relates to expected completion or delivery dates.
- administrator – someone with a knack for keeping records and documents in shape, who ensures that reports are done in time, and so on.

There are many views about the skills and characteristics that go into a well-balanced team. One very widely accepted list of team roles was developed by Meredith Belbin (1981), and the roles shown in Table 7.1 are based on his work. In a recent book, Charles Handy (1990) suggests that a team needs four basic types among its members: the captain, the administrator, the driver and the expert.

Whatever the particular mix, the point being emphasized here is that teams are best when made up of many diverse skills and talents. This diversity is potentially a source of great strength, although it may seem disruptive in the early phases of a project, until the varied members have learned to value the contributions each can bring.

Notepad

- *Take one of the lists of the roles a project team's members should ideally have.*
- *Evaluate the team you are working in at the moment against these characteristics.*
- *Which roles are well represented, and which are missing?*
- *Has that affected the way the team has worked?*

What are the danger signals?

Not enough team members

The manager may have trouble getting enough people released to work on the project team:

Table 7.1

Team member	Team role
Coordinator	He or she would rather be called disciplined and balanced than expert or creative for it is their job to pick the people, to listen and encourage, to focus and coordinate effort.
The shaper	The task leader, outgoing and forceful. His or her strength lies in the drive and passion for the task. He or she is needed as the spur for action but can be impatient.
The ideas person	The source of original ideas and proposals, he or she is a creative and intelligent member, but can be careless of details.
The critic	Better at analysis than creativity, he or she will do the checking and point out the flaws in the argument.
The networker	The popular extrovert contact person, someone who keeps the team in touch with the world around it.
The implementer	The practical organizer and administrator who turns ideas into timetables for action.
The team-builder	Likeable and popular, the team-builder keeps everybody going, by encouragement, understanding and support.
The finisher	Without the finisher the team might never meet its deadlines. The relentless follow-through is important but not always popular.

One of the main drawbacks was that commissioning staff could have been supplemented by skilled professionals from within the company, but this was denied to me as project manager. This threw a heavy strain and responsibility on myself and my assistant. It put me in a position of high stress, as I knew that the future of the company rested upon the successful outcome of this project.

Even when a person has been committed to the team, there is a constant danger that they get pulled back to other work:

The team member from Z wrote to me indicating that he's been asked by his boss to take on a new and urgent programme. Because his particular group is very short in resource, he will not be able to support this team. From my point of view that is totally unacceptable, as without a representative from Z, any solutions we come up with will be only partially successful.

The manager leading the refinery team experienced a similar problem:

> One disappointment (and, I believe, a significant factor in the project) was that just before commissioning, the manager of the pilot plant development team was transferred to another job. He had been promised to me at the project inception, and I had designed him into the working operation.

The ever-present threat was summed up by the manager who said:

> I've got to check every day that they're still working on my project.

Ineffective working

Staff from different professions or national backgrounds, or even simply from different operations of the same company, operate in different ways. Some will have a tendency to openness and creativity in solving joint problems, others will tend to stay within their area of special expertise.

Some may not be able to cope with the speed and intensity of the work, or with the forward-looking, often 'conditional' and unpredictable nature of project work. Others may not be natural team-players, so that when difficulties arise in the team, as they inevitably do, they withdraw rather than come forward.

One of the audio-diarists, a project leader in a multinational, drew attention to the practical communications problems between team members in widely separated places. His part of the design team had not been kept in touch with design changes elsewhere in the project, leading to extra work having to be done. He later observed:

> Communication, especially in an international setting, is extremely critical. Not only can strategy be understood, but technical problems can be solved rather than prolonged. Also undesirable political situations are more likely to arise due to poor communication.

Opposing coalitions

The team may become the outlet for opposition. It became clear to one project manager that coalitions were being formed at steering group meetings. Line management representatives formed an alliance, and offered different approaches to the project from those being put forward by the project sponsor, and by the manager who was implementing it. The latter overcame this by arranging for information to reach the sponsor that delays were being caused by the line managers' tactics. The sponsor then attended a couple of the meetings, and forcefully backed the project manager's line.

Competing demands

The project task will be competing against other demands for the time and energy of the team members. Departmental or business unit pressures will always be part of the team members' thinking, and will influence what they do and say more than the wider interests of the project as a whole. The project team or task is a temporary job; their career lies elsewhere.

This is a particular problem towards the end of a project. There is likely to be a great deal of tidying-up and finishing off to be done, in preparation for handing the project over to those who will be running it thereafter. Project staff are likely to be keen to move on to new tasks, which appear to offer more interest and challenge. Maintaining the team is as important for the tidy completion of a project as the original building and selecting.

Team-building skills for project managers

A team is not a committee, nor is it people gathered together to listen to a talk. It is a group of people who share some common objectives, and who are working together to achieve them. Merely assigning people to work with others on a project does not create a team: they may not share common objectives, and may not work together to achieve them. It is up to the project manager to turn those assigned or recruited to the task into an effective team.

Stages of team development

A team that becomes effective goes through identifiable stages of development – sometimes very rapidly, sometimes with great difficulty. The stages overlap, and are not as distinct as they appear in print – but having a sense of the different stages helps to assess where the team is. In his *Team Development Manual*, Mike Woodcock (1989) outlines four stages through which teams may grow:

1. The undeveloped team
This is the stage at which people have been assembled to work on a task, but have not yet given much thought to how they should work effectively together. Members are not asked if they feel committed or enthusiastic about the task; there

is much talk but little listening; little effort to reach a shared understanding of what needs to be done; and mistakes or difficulties may be covered up. The 'team' is not a team, as the hidden strengths and talents of the members are not being used.

2. The experimenting team

The distinguishing characteristic of this stage is that the team makes a conscious decision to review the way it works, so as to find ways of improving its performance. The team begins to experiment, to face problems openly, and to consider options widely. The values and beliefs underlying the options begin to be debated, more personal issues are raised, feelings about the task are expressed, and seen as legitimate matters for discussion. More listening takes place, and a wider range of contributions is considered.

3. The consolidating team

In the previous stage people learn to be more open; here they create clearer and more methodical ways of working. Rules and procedures are introduced, not as things that are imposed from above, but as improvements agreed by the members. Attention is given to such matters as:

- Clarifying the purpose of a task or activity.
- Establishing targets and standards.
- Collecting information that will be needed.
- Deciding what will need to be done.
- Turning that into a detailed plan.
- Reviewing progress, and learning lessons for the future.

4. The mature team

This combines the openness of the experimenting team with the method of the consolidating team. Flexibility is the distinctive feature, with procedures being used in different ways, depending on the task in hand. Leadership changes with the situation, formal management hierarchy may be abandoned in favour of a more appropriate structure. It becomes confident and outward looking, able and willing to take account of the wider aspects and implications of what it is doing. These are more difficult to handle, but team members are confident they have the skills to cope with them.

How can a manager, in any situation, help a team to move relatively quickly through these stages? Table 7.2 contains some suggestions.

Ideas for action

There are several things a project manager can do to get the benefits of a diversified team, while minimizing the problems and disadvantages.

Table 7.2

Stage 1

    Demonstrate openness by example
    Invite members to share their concerns and problems
    Encourage consideration of individual strengths and weaknesses

Stage 2

    Encourage greater openness
    Involve team members in reviewing team performance
    Allow conflicts and grievances to surface
    Question decision-making and problem-solving methods

Stage 3

    Agree procedures and methods of working
    Practice using those methods, especially in objective setting
    Develop the habit of regular reviews, to identify ways of continuously improving
    team methods

Stage 4

    Build bridges with other teams and units
    Allow leadership to change with the task
    Expose the team to external scrutiny

Based on Woodcock (1989).

Choose the right people – if you can

Getting the right people on the project is fundamental – but the manager will not always have the luxury of choice. The team may already be in place; there may be existing staff who cannot be moved; a department's nomination may be unchangeable.

To the extent choice does exist, remember that a project team should ideally have content, process and control skills. It is not sufficient to rely on having a team leader who is skilful at all aspects – though that helps. The skill needs to be more widely present, and it may be worth including some people in the team primarily for their process skills, for example.

A good procedure is to check that all the relevant content and control aspects are covered, and then, before finalizing membership, check the process aspects. For example, do those being proposed have enough time and commitment? If not, you may prefer someone who is less skilled in task terms, but who would more than make up for that in their ability to exercise process skills. Other points to note are the following:

- Numbers can be kept down by rotating membership, with people moving in and out of the team as relevant.

- Regard any list of team members' characteristics as a list of targets, a guide to use in putting together a team, not as a set of mechanical rules.

Consider whether to include in the project team some of the key stakeholders, especially those from outside the organization, such as banks, customers or suppliers. It depends on the scale of the project how best to relate the range of stakeholders (see Chapter 4) to the project team. If they are few, then they could well be represented on the project team; but if large numbers are involved, the project team would become unwieldy. Provided the team recognizes stakeholder interests, direct membership or representation is not essential. Another route is to invite them to join the broader steering group; the danger with that approach is that if too many interests have to be 'publicly' satisfied on the steering group, progress will be too slow.

Negotiate time for the team

A fundamental team management skill is to negotiate, and keep reconfirming, enough time for the team from their departments. This is essential, so as to ensure the project agendas are given enough attention and worked through. If members' attention and energy is diverted to problems back in their department, rather than being concentrated on the project, progress will be slow. Awkward problems will be ignored, and will then get worse.

One way to maintain the commitment of other departments or functions to release staff to the project is to show them evidence of progress. Especially valuable are tangible and immediate benefits which the department has received from the project, however small. This helps convince sceptics that the project is not wasting their resources.

Generate excitement

Try to get the project team's efforts off to a strong start. If they are from distant parts of the company, working on a high-profile project, arrange a special event with a top management presence, to generate a sense of excitement and indicate top management commitment. A development group had experienced several setbacks in the projects it had worked on, and morale was low. Changes in corporate policy and structure meant that new opportunities were appearing, and it was vital to rekindle the development group's enthusiasm:

The new director travelled to the plant with the local manager, so that the new strategies could be sold to the local engineers. Obviously there was initially a feeling of 'here we go again, another change'. However, as the meeting progressed with the group as a candid two-way discussion, attitudes changed. It was obvious that the new director was willing to accept inputs from the staff, and he was displaying a lot of trust in them by agreeing to give his most important development project to the UK group. Team work was the new message.

New tasks have been agreed for the engineers, and these have now been initiated. Both engineers have eagerly produced plans and schedules for completion of their responsibilities on this task. The fact that both are now working long hours at their own instigation suggests that the corner has been turned, and that we are now getting 100 per cent commitment.

Perhaps the major change to result from top management's interest and commitment in the local group is the change in attitude towards the more mundane tasks that arise from time to time. These are now in progress, whereas previously they would have been put off.

The same idea can be applied to smaller projects – some activity, presentation, brainstorming session, to mark the start of work, and to raise the profile of the project with team members and their departments.

One manager took a more individual approach. During the time immediately after the formation of the team, there were still problems of motivation. He therefore adopted the method of having a one-to-one discussion with each team member, highlighting the benefits of the project, and comparing it favourably with others in the department:

> The approach in each case was tailored to suit the individual, but was kept light-hearted, in keeping with the underlying culture in the department. In some instances, where the project leader's influence has not been sufficient, the organization's hierarchical structure was used to get work completed.

'What's in it for me?'

Changes or uncertainty caused by wider changes in policy, or changes elsewhere in the organization, sap the morale of project staff, and the project manager needs to be active in keeping commitment high. One manager realized his team of engineers were frustrated by delays to a project they were keen to work on, which meant they were having to do less challenging jobs. They were likely to leave if nothing was done – so their manager negotiated a separate set of tasks for them, to maintain their interest.

If problems arise, show that they are being taken seriously, take visible action to try and solve them – and let everyone know they have been solved.

The director has visited the UK three times in the year, which serves to demonstrate to the local staff his obvious interest, and the fact that their services are required and are valued.

Acceptance is easier to obtain if the people involved have something to gain. One manager running a project that needed the support of other managers took care to identify deliverables that were of personal significance to each of them. He ensured each was dominant in the project at the time when that manager's support was most required.

Face up to disagreements

Conflicts and disagreements are bound to arise between team members – over interpersonal problems, departmental interests or differences of opinion over the way the project should go. This is to be expected, given that the job is probably novel and uncertain, and yet at the same time the team is under pressure for results.

Time and patience provide one way of resolving them. This is where process skills become essential – confront the issue, set aside an uninterrupted period of time, and work through the disagreements. Decide, as usual, what your objectives and targets are for the meeting, and plan your behaviour accordingly.

Sometimes a brisker approach will be needed. One man was developing a performance reporting system, assisted by a steering group of three senior managers. They all had their own idea of what the report should be like:

> In order to overcome this I took the initiative and, working to the brief, designed a set of reports and a system specification that I put forward at the next Steering Group meeting. The three managers pushed for their own measures, but the positional and personal power of the Development Director overcame their resistance and brought agreement.
>
> On subsequent meetings, when challenged about the approach, I continually referred back to this meeting, at which they had agreed to the Development Director's proposals. In other words, I used the combination of prior agreement and proxy positional power to overcome the positional power base of the senior managers.

Publicize success

Remind the team of their successes – and make sure they are widely publicized. Problems and difficulties always attract attention, and are quickly talked about around the organization. Balance that by ensuring people know about the successes, the work done, the progress made – and about the team responsible.

A project team had been severely hampered by lack of skilled resources from the plants taking part. To the manager's surprise, progress suddenly began to be made:

> The team was joined by a new hire, who had been involved in this aspect of the business in the States. He has made a great difference to the resolve of the team to move forward, even though the membership is a bit patchy. They have now come up with a rough idea of how they will do the task, and are preparing a presentation. I must confess I am delighted by this degree of progress.

Keep looking outside

A danger facing enthusiastic, committed teams is that members forget those outside the team. Yet ultimately it is they – senior managers, colleagues, staff and ultimately customers or clients – who will judge whether it is successful. This implies that the team needs to develop the habit of remembering these outside interests, and managing them properly. At the earlier stages, this means ensuring that the objectives and success criteria which the team develops for the project still meet the needs of sponsors or other interested parties. It means building good relations with key groups outside the team – and perhaps treating some, for example major suppliers, almost as members of the team. It also means being alert for clues, hints and rumours about the needs and concerns of those who are outside – but who will affect or judge the team's success.

Use high-performance methods

Several techniques can be used on a day-to-day basis to keep a project team performing well. These include the following:

- **Short meetings.** Hold regular meetings, say weekly, at which all interested parties are present. These can be used for strategy and planning, but also to keep everyone up to date with the progress of each other's work. One company has daily meetings on some fast-moving projects, limited to fifteen minutes. Experience has shown them that if they are kept short, people do not see them as a chore, turn up, stay on the subject and enhance productivity.
- **Ensure the targets are understood.** Since the project team is probably drawn

from people with different backgrounds, they will have different expectations of what the project is intended to achieve. Take time in the early stages to ensure common understanding of the remit.

- **Keep promises.** If promises are made to the team about facilities, staff, information – make sure they are kept:

> The local manager had agreed with the director the acquisition of workstations and software to support the project. Systems were installed exactly two weeks after this date, and this was a visible confirmation of upper management support.

- **Provide physical support.** Make sure the team's physical working environment support them. Provide an office where they can meet easily, in good working surroundings. This also gives a tangible signal that the project is being taken seriously by management, as well as providing a convenient place to leave messages or collect information.
- **Communicate well.** Fast and regular communications are vital to commitment, especially in projects linking several parts of the organization. If sub-groups are formed, or if members miss meetings, what arrangements are there for keeping them all in touch with each other?

  Make sure minutes of meetings are prepared quickly – preferably the same day as the meeting, and circulated immediately. These should be formal, and clearly show what action steps were agreed, and who was to be responsible for what. The same goes for other paper and documents, and anything that keeps people up to date with changing circumstances.
- **Technology can help.** Modern communication methods can also help overcome the problems of dispersed project teams. For example, senior managers can involve the local managers in staff meetings through a conference call facility on the telephone system. Email or fax can speed up links with remote sites, ensuring they do not feel out of touch with fast-moving changes.
- **Maintain management links.** However committed and enthusiastic the team gets about its work, it is vital that it is subject to scrutiny and support, through the creation and maintenance of good links into the management structure. If the project is complex and lengthy, the team may become so immersed in their own system that they lose touch with wider policy changes. Conversely, senior management, having set up the project, may become preoccupied with current issues and lose touch with the direction being taken by the team.

  To overcome this danger, establish a clear reporting link, either directly to a senior manager, or through a steering group. This ensures that senior management can monitor and control the general direction of the project, and that project effort is concentrated on critical areas. It also helps if you can engage the interest of someone in a powerful, authoritative position, who can act as a bridge between you and senior management. Having built the link, make sure it is used, by providing regular information on progress.

This also lets the team know that what they do and achieve is made visible to senior management, is seen as important, and has their interest. It is also a useful way of ensuring that there are fewer erratic changes in goalposts, and that links are made at a high level between the project and changes going on elsewhere in the organization.

Personal checkpoints

- Review how the team has been working on the project so far. Is it an asset to the job, or are there weaknesses?
- Raise the issue of how the team works at the next meeting, ensuring some time is made available to reflect on progress so far, and to identify practices that have helped the team to perform well, and those that have hindered it.
- Decide, with the team, what you will all do about those that are hindering progress.
- Which roles seem to be underrepresented on the team? What will you do to put that right?
- Review the links between the team and the management structure, to ensure they are adequate.

8

Managing the staff

Involving staff and users

Project managers have to bring people along with the changes they are making. A sense of involvement has to be created amongst those who will be working or using the new systems and procedures long after the project team has moved on.

The most visible group are the people whose work is directly altered by the change, and who will be living with the results in their daily work. They have to set up the system, and run it thereafter. They have a direct interest in the change, and detailed operating knowledge of the situation. These are assets which the project manager would be foolish to ignore.

Managers in charge of the area where the change is taking place should also be considered. Their status and working relationships may be affected, and they will need to keep things running while the change itself is introduced.

Finally, there are those who receive the results of the work done in the area. These can be members of the public, customers, suppliers or people in other departments. Their link to the change may be slight – but ensuring that they know what is happening avoids confusion and misunderstanding at a difficult time.

These groups will probably have been identified in a stakeholder analysis: this chapter shows how they can be managed, so that the assets are used during the project. The themes are as follows:

Using experience in planning change.
Gaining acceptance of change.
What are the danger signals?
Involvement skills for project managers.
Ideas for action.

Using experience in planning change

Having staff participate as fully as practicable in the design and implementation of a change ensures that it takes account of the practicalities of their job. All the issues making up the content agenda need to be handled. As Chapter 9, 'Managing the content agenda', makes clear, the range of matters to be dealt with is usually wider than expected. The framework shown there includes:

- **Technology** – sometimes in the physical sense, when the project involves new equipment or facilities. This heading also includes other substantive issues, such as the correct technical design of a payment scheme or operating system, when that is the focus of the project.
- **Structure** – including changes in the management structure, in management style or in career development opportunities. These items include a host of other issues, such as the boundaries between functions, the creation of reporting links, the relative status of departments, and performance measurement and review procedures.
- **People** – decisions are needed here about how work is to be organized for individual members of staff, and for groups of staff or work-teams. What the operating methods and practices are to be, how staff will be trained, and what they will be trained to be able to do. How to ensure they understand how their task fits into the whole picture, and their willingness and capacity to initiate further change.
- **Task** – in addition, of course, there are issues concerning the task to be done, the objectives that are set, and the targets or standards to be achieved. Often the most difficult aspect of a project is that of ensuring that clear objectives are set and communicated to those concerned.

Faced with this range of issues, the job of the project manager is made a great deal easier if he or she is able to draw on the skills and experience of the staff in the area. They know what the equipment needs to be able to do, how new systems would need to fit in with old, how the transitional problems could be handled.

One of the audio-diarists recalled that a successful feature of his project had been the decision:

> To involve local supervising management in route planning, which introduced and involved them at an early and critical stage in the project, and we were able to benefit from their local knowledge and experience.

Important aspects of an operation are easily missed – especially the new, unusual, uncertain or occasional elements. These can only be captured if staff and designers work closely together. Expectations will also be more realistic – consulting staff allows them to form a balanced view between what they would ideally like from the change, and what they are likely to get.

There may also be transitional problems to handle, such as transferring records. One of the diarists ran a project to introduce a computer-aided design system:

> A huge problem exists with the building up of an organizational database,

with something like 30,000 drawings currently existing, and it would take far too long to transfer those into the database by hand.

When systems go 'live' many small problems occur. If staff have not taken part in creating the system they will not 'own' it, and small problems will be allowed to grow out of proportion. Enabling staff or users to be part of the design process is likely to ensure that better decisions are taken about the details of the change to be introduced.

Notepad

- *What are the key 'content' issues which you think will need to be handled in designing the change?*
- *What sources of information and ideas are you aiming to use in planning the change?*
- *What knowledge and experience do current operating staff have which could help the project?*

Gaining acceptance of change

A change imposed from above will not be accepted as readily as one to which staff have contributed. There will be initial mistrust and scepticism – this needs to be turned rapidly into broad support, or at least constructive criticism. People will then be committed to sorting out the problems that will arise later. One man commented:

> The staff competency, training and morale were excellent. We had a small, tightly knit team who worked well together, who gave a great deal under very difficult circumstances. This, I believe, stemmed from my own role and that of my immediate subordinate, in establishing a positive atmosphere whereby we would not accept failure, but would carry on until we achieved success.

Staff may express anxieties and nervousness about a proposed system – if they can examine and question, they will be less uncertain, less apprehensive. One of the audio-diarists who was introducing a management information system was well aware of this uncertainty, and worked to overcome it, by involving staff in the design and specification process:

> If they are to feel that they are still on top of their job, and that job has changed a lot in recent years, they have to be actively part of the development process.

Major changes depend on staff being able and willing to put in a lot of extra work during the changeover:

> We encountered very significant difficulties in the first three months, with fouling and blocking of process lines, loss of solvent, wastage of product, etc. These were difficult days for everyone concerned, since it involved working almost continuously at the refinery. Even the younger men found it difficult to maintain attention and enthusiasm.

Momentum and interest has to be maintained in the aftermath of the change. Staff need to learn how to use the new system to full advantage, further organizational changes may be needed if the full benefits are to be realized, and the change will be refined in the light of experience. Such pressure will be more readily accepted when staff have been well managed earlier in the project.

Notepad

- *Which groups of staff need to accept the change and give it their commitment?*
- *What practices have you seen used that could be helpful in gaining their acceptance?*
- *What practices have you seen that were unhelpful?*
- *What plans have you at this stage about how to get staff commitment?*

What are the danger signals?

The project manager can be alert to signals that staff lack enthusiasm for the change. Overt and prolonged resistance is rare, but indifference and reluctance can be just as damaging to a project. It takes many forms, disguised or overt, including:

- Refusing to use the equipment or system.
- Deliberate misuse of the system.
- Using the system as rarely as possible.
- Maintaining old procedures.
- Delaying other changes necessary for a system to work.
- Missing meetings about the change.
- Making no effort to learn how to use it.
- Not releasing staff for training.
- Excessive fault finding and criticism.
- Endless discussion and requests for more information.
- Suggesting new features, which make the change more complex.
- Bringing other interest groups into the discussion, delaying agreement.

Any of these symptoms, if present, will result in the new system performing below expectation.

Notepad

Knowing why staff are reluctant enables the project manager to plan how to respond. Consider the following questions:

- *Have you observed any signs of resistance on this or previous change projects?*
- *Which of the symptoms above were shown?*
- *How powerfully were they expressed?*
- *What do you believe lay behind the resistance?*
- *How was it managed?*
- *What are the implications for the project manager?*

Involvement skills for project managers

A critical issue for the project manager is how to ensure that staff and users feel they have put their ideas and experience into the design of the change. Allowing users to partipate in the change process is widely predicted to produce changes that are better, and that are more likely to be accepted by staff – though hard evidence that these consequences actually follow is difficult to find.

One explanation of the link between user participation and project success is that it helps to maintain users' sense of control over their work. The argument is that in the normal course of events, in reasonably predictable working situations, staff and users come to exercise some degree of control and influence over the task. The work itself becomes familiar, expectations are established, rewards are fairly predictable, status is established, social relationships are worked out.

A change threatens all of this. Fearing a loss of control, staff become apprehensive or antagonistic towards the change, with all the negative consequences for the change, and for the staff themselves, which that entails. Elements of the situation which bring about this reaction are:

- Change – differences in the objective features of the old and new situations.
- Contrast – differences that are personally significant to those affected (some staff may welcome a feature, others dislike it).
- Surprise – significant differences between what was expected to happen, and what does happen.

This analysis leads to the proposition that acceptance of change will be helped by implementation activities that enable users to cope with change, contrast and

Table 8.1

Element	Activity
Change	Staff briefed in a discussion format.
	Staff actively take part in system demonstration.
	Demonstration designed to highlight not features, but what users would see.
Contrast	Staff able to discuss in small groups what the change might mean.
	Staff able to express personal anxieties about the change.
	Staff given degree of choice over when or whether they personally had to be part of the change (e.g. by making transfers available).
Surprise	Implementation staff present at meetings, to ensure accurate information is passed out.
	Staff told in advance about surveys, visits from consultants, deliveries of equipment, etc.
	Staff given significant influence over working methods and aspects of change design.

surprise – thus helping them maintain an acceptable degree of control. Practical possibilities include activities to deal with each of the elements, as in Table 8.1.

The underlying purpose of such practices is to enable users to retain their sense of control during the disruption caused by the introduction of major change.

Ideas for action

Action to gain the ideas and commitment of staff can be aimed at both the content and the process aspects of the change – what is done, and how it is done. Experienced project managers say that work to produce positive commitment has to begin early. Staffing issues should not be left aside until the technical problems have been solved.

Content

The project manager needs to recognize that staff have diverse attitudes, preferences, skills and interests. They will value different things at work; whatever these are, the project manager will have an easier time if he or she identifies benefits that staff value. These will be more persuasive than an approach which only stresses the features and broad objectives. The change has to be marketed to staff, in terms they will recognize:

The other major factor used in persuading staff the system was worth using was the knowledge of another system, which calculated a bonus for branch staff if they reached certain profit targets. The system we were proposing would help them improve their sales and thus their profit by focusing their attention on particular areas on a weekly basis. This would help improve their chances of meeting targets, and earning a bonus.

One of the audio-diarists reported on a successful change which followed a similar approach. Asked to identify decisions which helped the project, he replied:

To increase bonus performance levels where possible, which acted as a carrot to the manual workers, as it provided the opportunity to earn more money;
The staff were given four to six weeks to settle into the new method of operation, and to familiarize with their new routes. During this period their bonus levels were guaranteed;
To protect the loss of earnings for a period of nine months for the manual workers who became surplus to requirements.

Some people will be enthusiasts, others will feel unable to cope (and they may be right). Some will be eager and knowledgeable, others uncertain and defensive. The latter need time to adjust, and all will need some training to start performing.
A single training event for both types, unless done very sensitively, is likely to confirm the latter's fears rather than resolve them. Ensure the training itself is at the right level:

It was found that training given by the selling organization was pitched at experts, not beginners. Therefore specialist CAD trainers are required, with knowledge of the specific applications for which the equipment is to be used. Secondly, not all personnel are suitable to be trained for work on this type of equipment.

If training is done too early the system is likely to have changed by the time staff start to use it, and they will need to be trained again.
Some staff will fear losing their job, status or career prospects. These fears may be well founded – in which case they are probably best dealt with openly and early. Those who are secure can then concentrate on the job, rather than have it undermined by needless anxieties.
Expectations need to be managed, in the sense of being cautious about what the system will do and when it will be available. Loose promises are commonplace in early discussions about a project. Avoid justifiable scepticism by double-checking before ideas and time-scales are released to staff.
Staff will be more committed if the change seems likely to work. This implies

taking care over the design and planning of the technical aspects of the change – whether of equipment, procedures, or systems:

> Members of the project team, from past experience, suggested that although staff in the branch network were very enthusiastic about the new system, they would probably lose interest and not use it. The problem was to get them to accept ownership of the system.
>
> This was tackled by ensuring that the system was as simple as possible to use, and by providing full help facilities. In addition each region was asked to nominate a representative who would act as coordinator for their region. This person would receive advance training, and would be responsible for allowing access to the system by their region. It was their data to do with what they liked.

If the system is seen to be complex and difficult to use, and a distraction from other work, staff will distance themselves from it as far as they can.

Things to watch

Rewards
Anxieties about ability
Training
Security of jobs and status
System quality
Budget
Quality of jobs
Power changes

Users are right to resist a change that will do the organization more harm than good. Double-check that the system proposed will do the job. Set up test or pilot systems and take the lessons into account when putting in the full system. Pilot systems may be unrepresentative of the final situation, so interpret the results with care.

Change costs money, and staff will lose commitment if the budget for the change is inadequate, meaning that things have to be done on the cheap, making life more difficult for them. Check that the project time-scales are realistic, in view of the budget.

Change often means new patterns of working which take away valued parts of the role, or which alter the status or prospects of people and interests. It also creates a new form of power – staff can use their willingness to accept the change as a bargaining weapon in pay negotiations.

Try, as suggested in Chapter 6, to ensure that organizational changes are such that they provide quality jobs, or cohesive working groups, which complement the skills and experience of staff. Can the change be used to give people more information, so that they can make better decisions?

Manage power changes – consider whether changes in autonomy and decision-making really are intentional and do not come about by accident. You may need to negotiate acceptance of the changes with those groups or individuals whose power or organizational position is going to be diminished. You may also need to deal with those situations where change is being used for pay bargaining.

Notepad

Which of the headings in the box:

- *Are relevant in your project?*
- *Have been dealt with well?*
- *Need more work to get them right?*

Process

Gather ideas from staff

In any group there will be 'opinion leaders', who may not necessarily be the most senior people. Project managers can pay special attention to gaining the support and acceptance from these leaders for the change. The practices below all offer ways of using its experience of staff to gain their commitment, and to benefit the project.

- **Ask staff for ideas.** People become anxious when they do not know what is going on, or when they feel that their views are ignored. Encourage people to raise doubts and objections. If these are unfounded, they can be reassured; if they have substance, dealing with them will gain support.
- **Secondment to the project team.** This is a common way of ensuring that staff are represented – not just at the planning stage, but throughout the project. Remember that having staff representatives on the project team does not guarantee they will be effective. Do they transmit all requests from their colleagues, and do they take back all the relevant information? If in doubt, create other channels so that information reaches the staff directly.
- **Questionnaires.** These are an effective way of gathering views from a large number of staff about a proposed change programme, especially in the early stages. They give an overview of what staff want and expect from a change.
- **Individual discussion.** This allows you to check your understanding of what users anticipate from the system. It can, however, be time-consuming and you have to interpret the information given in terms of who gave it. For example, a manager may know what she or he wants from a change, but be

Ways of gathering ideas

Invite on to project team
Questionnaires
Individual discussion
Seminars and focus groups
Newsletters
Videos or video-conferencing

unclear on the detail of current methods. Junior staff may be clear on detail, but unaware of the wider processes.

- **Seminars.** To keep groups of staff informed about project progress, and cutting down on any secrecy about the change which might be developing. Staff will be able to ask questions directly, and the discussion itself will probably generate new ideas, and increase willingness to use the system.
- **Newsletters.** On large-scale projects, it will be difficult to arrange progress seminar for all users. To make sure that all staff are up to date, produce a project progress newsletter. In this way you ensure that the information you want to transmit goes directly to the users.
- **Modern technology.** Consider the use of video films as a means of sending a message widely and convincingly. An engineering company used this approach, to make a relatively traditional staff aware of the need for radical change, and to seek their ideas. A familiar television presenter set the scene, followed by a manager giving more detail on the company situation. The video allowed the same message to be given to staff across a large site, on different shifts, and was followed by local discussions on possible solutions.

Avoiding communication distortions

The manager of a management information project in a local authority realized that ambiguities were arising between what staff and potential users were being told by working party representatives and how the project was progressing in reality. The project managers decided that the best solution was to hold user seminars backed up by information sheets. The information sheets were sent directly to the staff, by name, a few days before the seminar.

Deal with snags quickly

If difficulties with the new system arise, do not just ignore them, or leave them for someone else to cope with in due course. For example, a utility company which experienced a lot of problems in adapting existing software to a new situation found this was beginning to undermine staff commitment. They adopted a deliberate policy of concentrating effort on to problem areas as soon as they arose, and told everyone what the problems were. They believed that this helped to reassure staff that their difficulties were being taken seriously and helped to maintain morale.

Publicize success

Bad news travels fast, whereas good news is taken for granted. Aim for some early victories, however small, and then make sure that everyone, including management, knows what has been achieved.

Continue to report the benefits being experienced, and how reluctant people would be to go back to the old system.

Moving a factory

The project manager of a move which had become rather controversial reported on the things he had done to gain staff support:

> The apparent changes in strategy had created a feeling of disbelief in some of the staff who will be obstacles to the move unless their opinions can be altered. The project manager must publicize the positive steps being taken towards the achievement of the move. Something we did was to use the informal network to put out the message that the furniture has been ordered, the new equipment is being installed, the desk layout is being drawn up, etc. This encouraged people by showing that finance was available, and that the change was happening.
>
> Another means to help the reality to become clearer was to allow some of the staff to visit the new premises, and let them see the partitions being erected, and the phone lines put in.

Manage the timing of participation

The timing of participation by staff in change is a tricky problem. 'As early as possible' is a common prescription, but this needs careful thought. Advantages of early participation include:

- You can replace rumour with fact.

- People have time to accept that the changes are going to happen.
- People are more enthusiastic at the start of a new project.

It may also be in line with a tradition of consulting with staff, which the project manager wants to follow.

To have extensive discussions with staff is, however, very time-consuming. Early involvement can also raise people's expectations and lead to disillusion if the project is delayed or postponed. So it is worth stressing:

- These are initial investigations.
- The projects may not happen.
- The change may not do all they want.

Personal checkpoints

- Identify the groups of staff on whose support you most depend.
- Check how much you know about their current attitude towards the project, and how that attitude may affect the outcome.
- Check how well the decisions being taken in other parts of the project will serve to gain staff support.
- Check how well the process aspects of the change are being handled, and how they are affecting staff commitment.

PART III
Wider aspects of managing change projects

9

Managing the content agenda

What needs to be done

The manager needs both to open the project up, and to close it down. Opening it up means ensuring that all the relevant substantive issues – the content agenda – are dealt with. It means ensuring that managing a change project is seen as a broad activity, rather than a narrow one. Equally, and simultaneously, the manager needs to be working to close the task down. This means ensuring that a vague problem, an ill-defined idea, is changed into a task that is clear and managable. It is about reducing uncertainty by defining the areas to deal with, and focusing effort.

This chapter provides a framework for handling these complementary requirements, of opening up and closing down. The particular issues on the content agenda will be unique. But the framework will show how to open a task up, so that the agenda covers the right areas; and how to close it down, so that work can be done. The themes are:

Items for the agenda.
Clarifying task objectives and benefits.
Developing solutions to support the objectives.
Bringing it in and handing it on.

Items for the agenda

Chapter 1 showed how to start setting the content agenda. Change usually involves dealing with four elements, shown in Fig. 9.1, and this very familiar diagram still provides an easy-to-remember guide to building a content agenda. A change in any one of these areas usually needs to be accompanied by a consistent or supporting change in each of the others. If this is not done, practice in these other areas is likely to be out of line with what is required.

So project managers need to check that each element is on the agenda, and that appropriate plans are made for them. The manager of one project which ran into grave difficulties recalled:

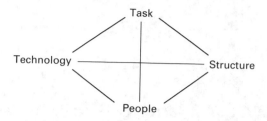

Figure 9.1   Elements of the content agenda

At this time, the end of 1986, the project was technically in good shape, although all the ramifications of by-product processing had not been worked out. However, the main products were of good quality, and were being sold, although market development for the by-products was slow, or in some cases non-existent. The capital demand for the refinery had been more than was budgeted for, and there was still a heavy capital programme to develop the refinery and to finish off many of the capital works which had been neglected in the early days because of the lack of money.

There were several organizational changes made by the new Operations Director. Things appeared to be settling down when it became apparent that the major problems that the company had to face were now almost entirely commercial: adequate markets could not be found for the main products, and more particularly for the by-products. These were accumulating to such an extent that . . . when the by-product tanks were full, the refinery had to close down until sales were made.

Reviewing this unsuccessful project, the manager later observed that amongst the factors contributing to failure were

the lack of market development activities . . . inexperience in getting to know the technology . . . lack of information about feedstock availability . . . our failure to maintain good relations with our suppliers . . . and the decision to deny key personnel the chance to work with the commissioning team on the refinery.

The project had been seen as primarily a technical matter, without adequate consideration of wider business issues – the content agenda had been set too narrowly.

Clarifying task objectives and benefits

Some projects are quite clear-cut in terms of what they are expected to achieve:

The Director requested the services of the Management Services Unit to implement this change throughout the city. I was assigned as project leader, to lead a team of management services officers in applying management services techniques to the review of present collection methods ... and to implement the changes.

and in cases like that, little time needs to be spent clarifying the objectives.

Other projects are less clearly set out, and the project manager is faced with a much less clearly defined problem. It may still be little more than an idea, which is being explored and developed before becoming a more visible proposal for action:

> This project is concerned with developing an enhanced computer system, 'to provide suitable performance measures'. This brief was not too clear, but attempts to clarify it proved futile, as the three senior managers all had their own ideas of what these should be – and they also had their own day-to-day activities to concern them.

In this example, the project is still vague and ill-defined, a messy problem with an unclear scope. The project manager has to judge how quickly to turn an open problem into a closed one. Do it too early, and opportunities for wider, more creative solutions may be prematurely closed off. Leave it open for too long, and people will become confused and impatient at the lack of direction.

Another early task is to make sure that the scope of the project manager's task is properly defined, and that everyone understands what it is. In the refinery example above, it could have been:

1. To manage the whole of the change, including the marketing and financial aspects.
2. To ensure the new plant is established as a working part of the organization, including the definition of work roles and responsibilities.
3. To ensure the new plant is established as a technically sound production unit.

With hindsight, it appeared that senior management saw the project manager's role mainly as (3), while he saw it as (2); and the project suffered from the neglect of (1).

Above all, project managers need to ensure that the objectives of the project, and the benefits expected, are clearly set and agreed at an early stage – even though they may change as new information becomes available:

> At that stage in the project, the long-term goal of the project was unclear to the team members. Some were implying that the required process was to be highly advanced, with no cost limitations, while others were proposing a system which used existing technologies, with minor modifications. It took several weeks of continual pressure before the product champion explained the goals of the project to the team.

It is easy to state an objective for a project, and assume that is enough. It

Figure 9.2   Steps in setting objectives

probably is not. Until objectives have been thoroughly thought out, written down and widely communicated, the project is in danger from:

- Vague problem definition.
- Expectations that are too high or too low.
- Targets that are vague.
- Conflicting priorities.
- Hidden agendas.
- Multiple goals appearing to be inconsistent.
- Misdirected effort.
- Confusion and poor commitment.

The benefits of spending time on objectives are, of course, the opposite of these, and include:

- Clear problem definition.
- Realistic expectations.
- Clear targets.
- High acceptance and commitment.
- Work achieves several objectives.
- Focused effort.
- People take initiatives consistent with objectives.

A method for achieving these benefits is to follow the five steps shown in Fig. 9.2.

Gather ideas

Most problems benefit from getting ideas from several points of view, especially when the project is novel and uncertain. A task that is novel to one manager may be familiar to another. Asking around for ideas and comments usually uncovers relevant experience about what is achievable. It reduces the uncertainty in the

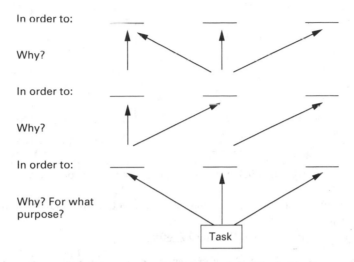

In order to:

Why?

In order to:

Why?

In order to:

Why? For what purpose?

Task

Figure 9.3 Framework for building a network of objectives

project manager's mind by providing information and ideas – about what others have done, what might be achievable, what areas to avoid.

By mentioning the possibilities of the project to interested parties, to the stakeholders, their ideas can be sought about what is proposed, and whether it is sound. They can be asked what it might achieve in their area and how it could relate to their objectives.

Take care to ensure that expectations are not raised too high – emphasize the provisional nature of the discussion, and that the project is still in its early days. As ideas firm up, it may be appropriate to have a more formal discussion with key groups to begin setting a clear set of objectives for the project.

Develop a clear set of objectives

A technique for doing this is to use a 'why/how network'. This makes it easy to see how several objectives fit together and support each other. Start by writing the name of the project in the middle of a large piece of paper, and then ask 'why?'. Answer by one or more sentences beginning with the phrase 'in order to . . .', and write these answers above the project task. For each of these answers, repeat the process of asking 'why?', and answering with 'in order to . . .', writing your answers on the sheet. Repeat this several times, until it makes sense to stop – usually when the objectives you are writing down are becoming very broad and long term (Fig. 9.3).

The diagram will need to be worked over several times to ensure all the main benefits are included, and that the right links are drawn between them. The method

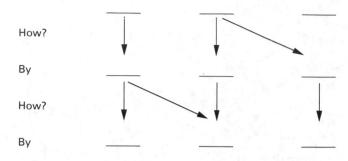

Figure 9.4 Framework for testing a network of objectives

can be used with other people working on the project, as this may help to make the diagram clearer.

This approach gives the following benefits:

- It shows how different objectives can be met – they may be complementary, rather than competitive.
- It demonstrates that short-term objectives (those near the bottom of the sheet) can help to achieve longer-term ones (those nearer the top).
- It tests whether the project objectives support wider organizational objectives.
- It gains commitment by showing how the project can meet several interests.

A way of checking the practicality or consistency of the diagram is to start at the top, and for each of the objectives shown there, ask the question 'how?', beginning the answer with the word 'by . . .' (Fig. 9.4). The words written below should provide a reasonable and practical answer to that question. If they do not, more work is needed on the diagram until the objectives are linked into a consistent pattern.

The diagram can be used in that form as a guide, or rewritten into a more conventional form, listing the short-term objectives of the project, and then the longer-term ones to which it will contribute.

Set measurable targets

It makes sense to ensure that reasonably measurable or observable results are set. Phrases such as 'reduce waste' or 'improve decision-making' are not precise enough, and are useless as a guide to progress. People are reluctant to make specific commitments in this area. That is understandable if a very novel project is being undertaken in a volatile business; in those circumstances it will be hard to know what is achievable, and there are risks in going public with an objective that could make failure visible. A natural urge to get into action will also cut down the time people are willing to spend. Setting any sort of objective is difficult enough –

having to set measurable targets for them looks like an added burden.

The project manager must persist on this point. Targets will let him or her provide clear and unambiguous information on progress or the lack of it, information which will be vital to credibility with senior management. Clear evidence of measurable progress can bring its own rewards to the manager. Equally, clear evidence of delay or difficulty can be used to make the case for additional resources, or for other supportive action by top management. It can also help to motivate a team or group of staff if they see results being unambiguously achieved.

Examples of quantifiable targets
- Deal with 95 per cent of claims within three days.
- Reduce departmental costs by 5 per cent within six months.
- Increase the proportion of repeat business to 60 per cent by 1993.

It is not always possible to quantify all the benefits, and some very important ones may be of this less tangible variety. These should be listed as well.

Examples of unquantifiable targets
- Avoiding duplication of effort.
- Maintaining a reputation for innovative service.
- Improve staff commitment to the organization.

Having a list of quantitative and qualitative targets dramatically reduces uncertainty on the project, by giving people something to aim for, and a measure with which to assess their progress.

Provide a vision of the end result

If the project is going to introduce significant changes, the project manager needs to help people to have a clear picture of what the changes will mean. Specific statements and examples are more useful than general impressions, and pictures or diagrams are more useful than words. Aim to give as clear a picture as possible of how the new situation will look to the people affected by it, or using it in some way.

For example, if the project concerns the introduction of a computer-based system, staff will probably want to know:

- What the screen will look like.
- What the terminal will look like.
- How the work area will be laid out.
- Where information will come from, and in what form.
- Where papers will be filed.
- How many others in the office will have the system.
- Whether they will be linked together.

Most of these can be shown in simple diagrams or pictures, and will give those concerned a much better picture of what the system could look like:

> We agreed that we should do a draft presentation, a very simple presentation, that would look at all our processes and systems, and then focus in on the scheduling project, in order to get the commitment we require. So we spent many long hours putting together an overall picture of how our order fulfilment systems could look in four years' time, and what would need to be done next year, and the year after . . . It was clear after about the first hour that we had managed to capture the interest, imagination and energy of the group.

The Lego factory

The project team planning a very large factory re-equipment project found a novel way of giving people a picture of what the end-result would look like. They set up a large table in their project area, and used Lego bricks to depict where each piece of machinery was likely to be. This allowed those working on the planning of services and material movement, for example, to visualize what the layout would be, and to point out the implications of different arrangements in very practical terms.

If people have a clear picture of the goal, they will be able to come up with their own ideas as the project proceeds. This improves project decisions, as well as commitment and ownership.

What makes a good set of objectives? They should:

- Use clear and explicit words and phrases.
- State targets, and be easy to imagine.
- Make a clear contribution to wider organizational objectives.
- Be a realistic result of this project.

- Be seen as feasible and attainable.
- Be accepted by stakeholders and interested parties.

Test for reality and acceptability

Throughout this difficult process, keep testing ideas both for reality and acceptability. The enthusiasm of those closest to the project has to be tempered by wider considerations in the business – competition from other projects, changes in business priorities, difficulties that turn out to be larger than expected.

Objectives only energize commitment if people accept them. In the early stages of a project, not all the interested parties will have come on the scene, and may not even be aware that the change is being planned. The danger here is that if a group has worked in relative isolation on the objectives, they may not be acceptable to others. Early exposure to a wide range of interests, with the opportunity to influence them, will usually pay off.

Notepad

- *How clear are you now about the objectives of the change?*
- *How will you use this method to help make these clearer to everyone connected with the change?*
- *Who may be able to help you through this part of the task?*

Developing solutions to support the objectives

The project described at the start of this chapter failed because the agenda was drawn too narrowly. It is not enough to establish the scope and objectives for a project. The project manager also needs to ensure that decisions in other areas form a coherent strategy which supports those objectives:

> One of the main worries from the operational managers is how this might affect the organizational structure, because it is quite a radical system, and obviously the technical and the organizational aspects have really got to go hand in hand for the best fit, not only for the department but for the organization as a whole.

Technology

Whatever the nature of the project, certain technical issues need to be resolved (Fig. 9.5). These may involve technology in the physical sense, as when the

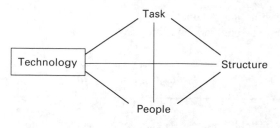

Figure 9.5

project involves new equipment; they may also involve other substantive issues, such as the design of a payment or job evaluation scheme, where that is the focus of the project. The details of the issues are specific to the project: Table 9.1 should

Table 9.1   The content agenda – technology

Areas to review	*(a)* *Relevant?*	*(b)* *In hand?*
Have needs and requirements been adequately specified?		
Have markets, customers, client expectations been clarified adequately?		
Does the proposal need to relate to existing systems and facilities?		
What are the likely ripple effects?		
What other current changes may affect this project?		
Adequate specification of physical facilities – technology, peripherals, space, communications?		
Suppliers, subcontractors, consultants, joint-venture partners thoroughly evaluated?		
Safety, health, environmental aspects?		
Financial evaluations prepared?		
Availability and terms of finance confirmed?		
Policies and operating procedures specified and designed?		
Compatibility with current or planned policies or common standards?		
Proposals tested, piloted, evaluated?		
Sensitivity analysis of options, risks, costs and benefits?		
Other items for the agenda		

simply be reviewed to check if any of these items should be included on your project agenda. Review the table, asking in each case whether the item is (a) relevant, and (b) in hand. Mark the columns to the right accordingly. This will indicate any areas where additional work needs to be done, to gather more basic data, or to devise solutions.

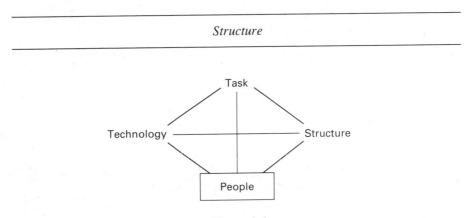

Structure

Figure 9.6

The content agenda needs to include any work required to deal with structural or organizational changes (Fig. 9.6).

If some new form of internal capability is required, this is best handled in the course of the project, not as an afterthought. Again the details will be unique to the project, but Table 9.2 indicates the areas to review.

For each item, the project manager should consider whether it is relevant, and then whether it is in hand, marking the appropriate space in the columns. Where an item has been shown as being relevant and in hand, an additional check is to mark the initials of the person dealing with it against the item. Make sure he or she realizes that.

People

Change is likely to require new kinds of working, and new relationships between people in different areas (Fig. 9.7).

These need to be addressed in the course of the project, not as an afterthought. Again the details of any solutions will be unique to the project, but Table 9.3 indicates the areas to review.

For each item, the project manager should consider whether it is relevant, and then whether it is in hand, marking the appropriate space in the columns.

Table 9.2 The content agenda – structure

Areas to review	(a) Relevant?	(b) In hand?
Management structure		
Areas of responsibility and authority		
Balance between local autonomy and central control		
Boundaries between functions and departments		
Reporting links		
Relationships with suppliers and customers		
Management style		
Organizational rules and procedures		
Organizational culture/atmosphere/task environment		
Relative power and status of individuals departments, interest groups		
Visibility of information on department performance		
Pay and reward systems, and other conditions of employment		
Career development		
Selection and training policies		
Career development policies and practices		
Performance measurement and review		
Other items for the agenda		

Notepad

List the main items from the technology, structure and people parts of the content agenda that you need to ensure are dealt with.

- *Who is going to be dealing with them, and how?*
- *How has this activity affected your overall picture of the scale of the project?*

Bringing it in and handing it on

However good the analysis of the items on the content agenda, the real test comes when the change has to be implemented. It is at this point that the quality of the

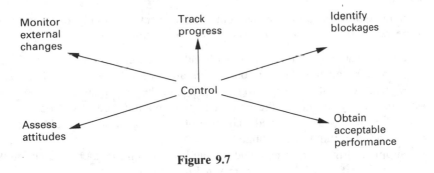

Figure 9.7

Table 9.3 The content agenda – people

Areas to review	(a) Relevant?	(b) In hand?
Work organization		
Staffing requirements and arrangements for different tasks		
The features and quality of individual jobs		
Organization of tasks within teams		
Operating methods and practices		
Availability of staff for jobs		
Ability to perform		
Availability of trained and experienced people		
Provision of training, and responsibility for it		
Interpersonal, cooperative and teamwork skills		
Understanding their task in the wider picture		
Understanding competitive priorities		
Willingness to perform		
Energy and enthusiasm		
Willing to learn new skills		
Capacity to initiate change		
Commitment to meet overall performance priorities		
Other items for the agenda		

planning shows up, as the plans come into contact with daily operating reality. Some points to consider at this stage include the following:

- **Phases.** There are often substantial benefits if the change can be introduced in phases, rather than all at once. This allows further testing and refinement, with difficulties resolved before going to the next phase.
- **Timing.** Try to choose the time of implementation carefully. Consider when holidays, peak workloads, absence of key people, etc., are likely to occur, and time things accordingly.
- **Support.** If the new system and the old have to run together for a period, how will staff cope? Can temporary help be hired?
- **'What if?'** List the things that are most likely to go wrong or cause difficulty. What contingency plans can be put in place?
- **Troubleshooting.** If difficulties do occur, staff commitment can be maintained if they see fast action being taken to sort things out. Make sure that resources can be made available at short notice to fix problems as soon as they arise.

Projects of the kind we are dealing with here rarely seem to be 'finished', in the sense that tangible construction projects are finished. Two things need to be remembered:

1. Time needs to be spent on bedding the change in, and ensuring that momentum is maintained. This can be lost in the closing stages, as the emphasis needs to shift to the details and the snags. Staff and management attention turns to newer and more exciting tasks, so the project manager has to keep driving the project through this hazard.
2. There has to be a clearly established responsibility for the maintenance and upkeep of the change after it has been implemented. The idea of things returning to 'normal' after a change has been introduced is an increasingly dangerous one – it needs to be someone's job to keep enhancing and developing the new system or procedure, in line with external events.

Personal checkpoints

- Check that the objectives you have developed for the project are still in line with those of senior managers, or other key external stakeholders.
- List the major uncertainties surrounding the project, and check that your work in this chapter has helped to reduce them.
- Ensure that all the critical items on the content agenda are someone's responsibility, and that they realize this.
- Check with stakeholders that they are aware of, and understand, the implications of the content agenda you now have.

10

Managing the control agenda

Keeping the change on track

Novel and uncertain projects need a new kind of control. Formal techniques are widely used to help control large and complex projects, by monitoring events against a project plan, especially those events that are relatively predictable and quantifiable. Novel projects entail managing less predictable, more uncertain, activities – where structured project control methods are of limited help.

This chapter will show how a change of emphasis within the control process gives a better picture of what is happening in major changes. This approach, using well-known interpersonal skills to gather softer, unstructured information about progress, can be used in addition to more formal systems of project control. The themes are as follows:

Why control?
Elements in the control cycle.
Controlling novel and uncertain projects.
Finding out what is going on.

Why control?

Control is a continuous monitoring process to keep variances acceptably small.

The audio-diaries showed that many of the managers' activities were directed at exerting control over the project. There were numerous examples of elements of the control process being used by the project managers – monitoring internal and external events, assessing whether they were helpful to the project or not, and taking corrective action if needed. This enabled them to do the following (Fig. 10.1):

- **Track progress.** Wanting to know when each phase had progressed to the

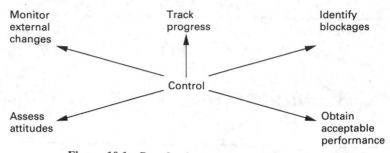

Figure 10.1 Benefits from project control

point at which the next ones could begin. Ensuring that the results expected were being achieved, in terms of time, budget, quality and acceptability – despite disruptive changes in direction and priorities.

- **Identify blockages.** The earlier these could be identified, the easier it would be to minimize delay. Anticipating trouble – such as important elements in the project being neglected, which would jeopardize progress later. The novelty and uncertainty of the changes made it hard to predict where these would be.
- **Obtain acceptable performance.** Project managers wanted to know whether people were meeting work targets, motivating their own staff, turning up to meetings, providing resources, releasing staff for training, answering queries and so on. If they were not, what clues did that give to the project manager about the priority being given?
- **Assess attitudes.** What evidence was there about the enthusiasm and commitment of those working on the project? Were there signs or hints of resistance, which might suggest a change of approach? Were staff becoming frustrated by delays, difficulties or changes to plan, which the manager needed to do something about? Or were they enthusiastic and positive about the activity, and going out of their way to make it work?
- **Monitor external changes.** The managers needed to be ready to react to unexpected changes changes elsewhere in the organization, or in the outside world, which had a bearing on the change they were introducing. Projects with wide links to other activities, in a volatile environment, experienced many such shifts, to which the project manager needed to be able to adapt.

Notepad

- *Which of these reasons for control are important to your project?*
- *What methods have you found useful in giving you the information you need?*
- *What problems have you had in keeping track of what is going on?*

Elements in the control cycle

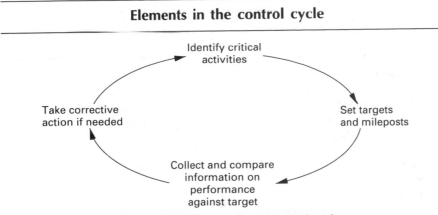

Figure 10.2 Elements in the control cycle

The planning and control cycle for any activity is represented in Fig. 10.2. The critical activities for those managing a change project will be those identified in the content agenda, in the process agenda and, of course, in the control agenda as well. Effective management of a change project depends on each of the three agendas being handled well, implying a process of monitoring and correction.

Targets for each critical activity can be set, using either quantitative or qualitative measures as appropriate. Then mileposts can be established, indicating what has to happen by when – when each of the activities needs to start, and when it needs to finish.

A chart like that in Table 10.1 can be prepared. The task of simply listing the activities (expanding the headings as needed) is a useful discipline. It serves to remind everyone of the main dimensions of the project, and often prompts the inclusion of forgotten items. It also gives a common visual focus for the project. Setting out these headings is itself a form of control – it prevents tasks from being overlooked, and helps people see what needs to be done in good time. There may still be disagreement about what is important and what is urgent – but at least the items are on the list.

If the project is large and complex, much more formal and structured project planning techniques will be needed, to keep track of the many elements and activities. Information on each has to be gathered and compared with what was intended. This structured information, whether from a manual or computer-based project management system, is vital to keeping the project manager up to date with what is happening. It enables corrective action to follow in response to signs of trouble.

Controlling novel and uncertain projects

Control systems only work if they reflect the task being controlled. The activities to be monitored, the information to be collected and compared, the form of

Table 10.1

Activity	Months						
	1	*2*	*3*	*4*	*5*	*6*	*7*
Content agenda							
Clarify task objectives							
Plan technological changes							
Plan structural changes							
Plan people changes							
Process agenda							
Identify stakeholders							
Establish roles							
Establish ownership and commitment							
Set up project team							
Plan communication strategy							
Plan consulting and negotiating							
Control agenda							
Key activities listed							
Agree targets and review dates							
Formal information systems established							
Informal processes agreed							
Review points agreed							

corrective actions need to fit the job. Here we are dealing with the novel and the uncertain, where structured control systems may not work.

In order to 'keep control', the project manager needs to be receiving and interpreting information relevant to the progress of the change. Some of this will be about physical, tangible or measurable aspects – has the design been tested or not? how did it perform? how much of the budget has been spent? and so on.

Other information will be about the attitudes and reactions of people to the change. Are staff going along with the proposals? How much commitment does there seem to be towards overcoming difficulties? Are there signs that people are having doubts about the wisdom of the project, but are not speaking out openly?

The project manager also receives information that is even more speculative – about impending events, possible changes in policy, proposed changes in another department, rumours of a competitor's move, reports about a likely technological breakthrough. Such information can help the manager to anticipate events that affect the project, to create opportunities, and generally to stay ahead of the game. The dilemma which this poses for the manager of an ambiguous project is clear. The project can only be properly managed with access to wide and uncertain information; but that range and uncertainty makes it extremely difficult for the project team to be able to plan its collection. Even if they could, much would require local expertise and knowledge to assess and interpret its significance.

This implies two things. First, that project managers need to be as receptive to 'unstructured' information as to traditionally structured information. Second, that they need to be willing to allow much more self-control on the part of those closer to the action – who know what the information means, and who have the ability to interpret and use it responsibly in the interests of the project.

The diary accounts illustrate the situation facing these managers in their attempts to keep control of their projects. One was introducing an order scheduling programme across seven European sites. He commented at one point:

In our company where every sector moves so quickly the business plan changes very quickly, is very volatile, the products change very quickly; it is enormously difficult to get people to focus on what is important rather than on what's urgent.

The Steering Group are getting together again in mid-November to discuss where we go from here. There are some problems that have arisen in the mean time that are worthy of note. This programme will primarily affect seven shipping sites. There are some interesting organizational and business discussions going on in each of these plants which have a bearing on this programme, and it may be useful to give the background to each.

A is going through a major increase in demand for its products, and this is having to be met without any increase in staff. Innovation is therefore required. Innovation takes energy, and the A management team are engaged in trying to meet this market demand and at the same time support my system. This puts a lot of stress on the system.

G on the other hand do not have such a high demand in their product sector, and therefore they are clearly in the position where they wish to drive improvements in their processes and systems in order to prepare for the time when demand for their product improves.

V is completely different again. They have just been introduced to the systems business, and are trying to get used to what it is like as a shipping plant, with all the pressure, all the customer service requirements being placed upon them.

C on the other hand have been in the business for many years, but are spread across three locations. Their motivation to support our programme is split down the middle. Half their business they handle on their own directly with the customers, and half is business that they need to work with us in order to supply the customer. We therefore have the problem of keeping the level of energy and motivation up across three sites, and in a business where only half the revenue is directly related to the activity we are trying to promote.

X is the most interesting of all. It is a large, but newly consolidated, business which has not yet established its own business model, and its own management team. They are a very important partner in this enterprise, and we have to make sure that their goals and objectives are set in such a way that they can support this programme, and that they are resourced to be able to do so.

What we have therefore is seven sites, three of which belong to the same business, and each of which has their own problems and are at different stages of their own development. We have to make sure that each of them is positioned in terms of energy, resources and commitment to support an integrated European programme.

At the November meeting he found that he had three major problems, two caused by sites not putting the resources into the programme that had been agreed. The third concerned site V where

the team member indicated to me that he's now been asked to do another European programme, basically around getting a product to the customer in seventy-two hours, and that as his group is very short of resource, he will not be able to support this team. From my point of view as a programme manager this is totally unacceptable, as without that plant, any solution we come up with will be only partially successful.

Another diarist recounted his work on the early evaluation of a proposed computer system:

Now what's happened is that acting from one of my reports the Director has decided that he is looking for a cost-justification for having the system at all, particularly now he's discovered what one of the options (Z) might cost. So really for the first time the 'do nothing' option is arising.

How best to tackle this? I decided that again I wanted to communicate with everybody who may be involved with this system, talk to them, try to identify the potential benefits at both area and headquarters level, so that we can have a full reflection of the management's requirements, both present and future.

So I've had a few meetings, there's a few more to go, to discuss benefits. The way that the rest of the business is developing their system, and the corporate policy on integration, means that we could at some point be forced to adopt option (Z), or something very similar, so there's no real doubt in my mind about why we should progress on this project. But I think a great deal of doubt arises in how best to fit, first of all, the existing computer system with the new computer system, and how the new computer system will fit this department, and this region's way of working.

Having evaluated all the options, I concluded that option (Y) was the best. The only problem was that option (Z) was politically more acceptable, and that the people least in favour of (Y) were the computer people, as they saw that it would weaken their power base.

The final example is from a project manager leading a team to develop a new product, again within a multinational business. He reported the stages in the project as follows:

A major strategic decision was taken by the company to enter this market, and I was put in charge of a small development team to design part of the new range. The project got off to a good start, and commitment and enthusiasm amongst the team was high.

After about a year, problems began to arise. Part of the work was being done by a partner with experience in this field, and it became clear that their system had serious deficiencies. Problems were increasing. Development plans were not as advanced as anticipated, and the system was not easy to use. It was definitely inferior to the competition.

At the same time the local team were suffering increased frustration, resulting from the difficulties encountered with the system, and the poor communications. When tasks were thought to be complete, the UK engineers would find that system software had been updated. This meant it would no longer run as anticipated, or it meant redoing the work completely.

These problems can be attributed to the lack of project management associated with the system software changes and lack of procedures to communicate these to appropriate parties. In addition the marketing strategy was about to be changed. All this combined to seriously affect morale in the local group. The US group was now in firefighting mode, and a number of organization changes were made in an effort to speed up progress.

The project went through several further changes in focus and organization, with associated effects on morale and commitment:

New projects were assigned to the UK, and these initially rekindled enthusiasm, which was soon to be dampened when it was realized that their functions were unlikely to be required by customers. Also problems were still being encountered with undocumented software changes, despite the fact that reporting procedures were now established.

Nevertheless, things began to get better, and after a further set of changes, he was optimistic about the future. Reviewing the lessons from the experience, he observed:

In a change such as this, details cannot be determined at the start of the project. Should management therefore be more realistic, and set less formidable goals?

Putting staff into smaller groups which were functionally complete, with a leader who believes in delegating power downwards in the organization, has helped to create a more effective and enjoyable environment to work in. Now the engineers are being encouraged to control their own schedules, a type of individual project management approach. This is seen to be more effective and more enjoyable for each engineer, creating a feeling of responsibility and commitment. It has helped to develop a sense of pride in the work delegated to individuals, and has been confirmed by the enthusiasm displayed in my own group.

From my own point of view, the ability to make decisions without having to go through long and laborious approval loops has significantly improved morale and productivity.

As we discussed in Chapter 2, novel and uncertain projects bring distinct

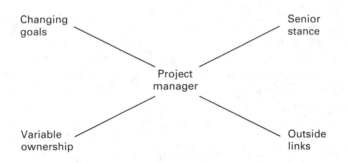

Figure 10.3   The context of the project manager

challenges for project managers, as shown in Fig. 2.3, repeated here (Fig. 10.3). Each of these features has implications for how projects can be controlled:

- **Changing goals.** Project managers were typically dealing with tasks where the goals were ambiguous, uncertain and liable to change. Goals were seen as having to be flexible and changeable, as business conditions and priorities inevitably changed in the course of long projects. In such projects, goals resembled broad targets or guidelines within which project managers were expected to operate. They were expected to do so flexibly, being willing and able to change as the business changed. This could imply a need to seek to combine the goals of different interests, rather than seeing them as competitors which needed to be eliminated; and an ability not to be restricted by linear thinking.
- **Senior stance.** The attitude and behaviour of senior managers can greatly affect the course of the project. Changes in policy elsewhere in the

organization, changes in priority or uncertainty about the direction of the business, all introduce additional uncertainty into the project.

- **Outside links.** Progress on their project often depended on parallel and consistent work being done in other departments or by subcontractors or joint-venture partners. In other cases, the project depended on other parties themselves making changes in their organization and systems. The project managers often had only tenuous authority in such situations.
- **Variable ownership.** Commitment of key people or groups to the project had to be worked for, and could not be taken for granted. A function may have been very supportive of a change when it was first proposed – only to find that changes in their own business priorities meant they could no longer provide backing for the project manager.

These elements, and the relationships between them, were themselves flowing and changing. The setting of the project was in a state of flux – a world of shifting patterns, rather than of fixed elements. Often the manager was controlling a series of independent, parallel activities, which were moving at different paces, but which needed eventually to come together.

Two other themes emerge from these accounts which are relevant to the control process:

1. **Systemic view.** The accounts highlight the importance of seeing the job as a whole, and of not concentrating exclusively on one dimension. They show how the several elements in the content agenda need to be kept in balance, and dealt with together. This perhaps indicated an ability to see the change project as a series of loops, not as something which moved in a single line; and an awareness that cause and effect were not always clear.
2. **A concern for process.** The project managers showed a clear awareness of the importance for process of gaining the commitment, enthusiasm and sense of ownership of the staff involved with the project. The diarists put much effort into the exercise of interpersonal and group skills, to influence others and to move the job forward.

These perspectives shape how the job can be controlled. Managing such a constellation of changes – ambiguous, uncertain tasks, in a dynamic context – cannot be done by a mechanistic approach to control. The high degree of unpredictability made it hard to specify in advance which elements should be controlled, and how this should be done. With so many forces beyond the direct control of the project manager, they could not hope to exercise total control over the situation, to dominate all that happens within the project.

Two approaches can be used to deal with this:

1. **Explicit open-endedness.** Recognizing the situation for what it is, and ensuring others do as well, by asking questions such as:
   (a) how can we publicize the level, and the sources, of the uncertainty inherent in the task?

(b) what can be done to reduce the uncertainty?

(c) do we have to decide z at this stage?

(d) should we plan to review the project objectives and assumptions in x months' time?

Addressing uncertainty openly means that staff are more aware of the situation they are in, and less likely to regard change simply as a sign of muddle (which of course it may be).

2. **Go with the flow.** While keeping the broad goal clearly in view, being ready to change direction somewhat, if the signals pointed that way. Being ready to:

(a) gather soft information;

(b) anticipate change – in plans and possibilities;

(c) take corrective action which changes the course of the project in the light of these external events.

An example of going with the flow occurred in the order-scheduling case set out above. Having prepared an initial proposal, this was put to staff from the seven sites who would be involved:

> The paper in general was well received. However, it was also clear that people were beginning to get a little bit sceptical about what it was actually going to take to enhance our internal processes and systems. Major pan-European redesign work had been attempted in the past . . . and had failed miserably, because the design team had produced solutions which were inappropriate, or were not accepted by each of the divisions.
>
> How then were we going to develop and deliver this programme which had to be done in an integrated European way? There was a feeling in the company that this was not the way to proceed. The team decided to get together again and work out a plan of attack. We spent many days convincing ourselves that the only way we could do this was on a European-wide basis. Our business was so integrated that it could not be segmented, and therefore had to come off a common rule base. We may, however, be able to develop the solutions independently as long as they were coming from the same base – a glimmer of light at the end of the tunnel, possibly.

This was the approach adopted, and he was able later to report that:

> It is because we have a business which is fairly complex and so diverse that we have adopted the approach that basically says: generate a common level of understanding of what needs to be done, then allow each area to specify their unique requirements within this overall framework. It also allows each individual unit to move at their own pace, as long as they don't exceed a maximum that we all agree – in this case, eighteen months.

Here we see a responsive control system in operation – sensing disagreement and doubt, and taking account of that information from the potential users of the system to revise the principle on which it was designed. This redesign would still be consistent with the overall goal of a more integrated order-scheduling system.

A similarly responsive approach was indicated in the semiconductor case. The original intention had been to enter market C – on the basis of an analysis which had concluded that the business 'must enter market C, or crumble'. This analysis proved incorrect:

> Some parts of market C have already turned into a cut-throat commodity business, with over a hundred vendors offering similar products. Prices have been driven down, and margins squeezed. At this point, products for market C represent less than 5 per cent of the company's business.

So although the company had experienced difficulty with the original product development strategy, it had been able and willing to alter that approach when it received signals from the market, and redirect the efforts of the project team to other areas. Again, control was used to monitor events and then redirect them within a broadly defined set of goals, rather than towards a narrowly defined and fixed one.

Notepad

- *How closely does your project fit the pattern of the examples here?*
- *How closely does the present control system fit the project?*
- *How well does it work?*

How should the conventional control cycle be used in novel and uncertain projects? What does this all mean for the practicalities of control? Clearly, external controls will help. These are the formal systems of rules, budgets, guidelines, checkpoints, mileposts and reporting procedures. Large and diverse projects depend on structured information about a wide range of events, not least to meet contractual and safety obligations. The project, described above, to develop a new electronic device, was shared between development groups in three widely separated locations. Each worked on different parts of the system, which needed to be consistent. At one point the manager of one of the development teams reported:

> The local team were suffering increased frustration, resulting from the difficulties encountered with the system, and the poor communications. When tasks were thought to be complete, the UK engineers would find that system software had been updated. This meant it would no longer run as anticipated, or it meant redoing the work completely. These problems can be attributed to the lack of project management associated with the system software changes and lack of procedures to communicate these to appropriate parties.

But a greater emphasis on internal controls will be needed. These place more reliance on the strength of shared norms and values amongst the group working on the project, and on individual self-control. The assumption is that, both consciously and unconsciously, strong commitment to the project can be created within individuals, and that a substantial part of the control process can then be carried out by them, exercising internal self-control over the project work. The control of ambiguous situations depends on generating a high degree of self-control amongst those involved in the project:

> Putting staff into smaller groups which were functionally complete, with a leader who believes in delegating power downwards in the organization, has helped to create a more effective and enjoyable environment to work in. Now the engineers are being encouraged to control their own schedules, a type of individual project management approach. This is seen to be more effective and more enjoyable for each engineer, creating a feeling of responsibility and commitment. It has helped to develop a sense of pride in the work delegated to individuals, and has been confirmed by the enthusiasm displayed in my own group.
>
> From my own point of view, the ability to make decisions without having to go through long and laborious approval loops has significantly improved morale and productivity.

This illustrates the idea of moving the emphasis in project management from control to commitment, through greater reliance on self-control. The approaches are not necessarily competitive. A large project will need both, to cope both with the scale of information required, and with the degree of ambiguity that is likely to be present.

A critical point is to ensure that the two approaches are consistent and mutually supportive, rather than pulling in different ways.

Notepad

- *What external controls are used in your project?*
- *How much reliance is placed on internal controls?*
- *What risks do you see in relying more on internal controls?*
- *How might these risks be reduced?*

Finding out what is going on

The key to effective control is the availability of information about what is happening in and around the project. From the earlier accounts by the project managers, it is clear that they needed to know about the following:

- Progress on the tangible, visible aspects of the project – the elements in the content agenda, and how those related to targets and milestones.
- Impending changes in policy, changes around the organization which would have a bearing on their project, and changes in the external environment.
- The attitudes and commitment of other managers, their staff and of key stakeholders – a range of 'soft' information, critical to the project's progress and acceptance.

Formal systems of project control have been developed to meet the first requirement. Where the activities and targets can be identified, specified, targets set, schedules drawn up, and where progress itself can be expressed in numerical terms, then a variety of systems exists. These range from simple manual systems, through more complex varieties, to those that are elaborate and computer-based.

Another valuable source of information to the control process is the use of carefully structured pilot installations, and the careful phasing of installations:

> We implemented area-by-area across the city, rather than trying to do it all at once. This led to tighter control as we were able to concentrate our resources to ensure quality project management. We also separated two aspects of the service and dealt with them separately. This enabled the pace of implementation to be dictated by the planning and progress of the various services.

Another project manager reported a similarly cautious approach, which in this case was in line with the culture of the company:

> The management style of the parent company filters down to the subsidiary, and leads to a tendency to make incremental changes. There is therefore a tendency to test the technology prior to large expenditure of finance. This led to the decision to choose a low-cost system.

Both of these can be contrasted with the refinery case, where it was reported that one of the factors in the failure was:

> the decision to develop all our own technology ... this was a mammoth task, which would never have been attempted by a major company.

Project managers also needed information about possible policy changes, and about staff attitudes. Formal systems were of little help in this, as the key information was unpredictable, and 'soft'. Much more reliance was therefore placed on obtaining it through frequent discussion, regular face-to-face contact, formal meetings and unplanned conversations:

> I had the review meeting on the 18th, and as a result of that meeting I have

two major problems ... though, in one case, they have now realized the need to do something, so they have all agreed to go away and each work on a bit of the project to the best of their ability. This is fairly unique for this group of people to feel so responsible for the future, so as to give up their time to help the project forward: so although it's a problem, it's progress.

In another case, the project had been initiated at the top of the organization, with the project manager briefed to look at the detail of what was proposed. He commented:

I was bound by the politics of the situation to communicate with operational management. So a great deal of time has been spent with them, describing the system, its objectives and finding how it might meet their needs. At this stage they seem to be a bit uncertain, a bit dubious. One of their main worries I think is how this might affect the organization structure, because it is quite a radical system.

After further work had been done, and new guidance issued from the top, he held further discussions with the operations managers, whose support was important to the project:

One interesting thing of note to come out of these meetings is that some of the managers feel a bit stunned with the rate of computer development work taking place in the company. They are more or less numb, and their reaction to what their requirements might be is – 'you tell me'.

Notepad

- *How do you know what the state of the project is?*
- *What are your most useful sources of information?*
- *What aspects of the change would you like to have more information about?*

Another manager was in the role of leading a development group of a project which was getting into difficulties. One of his key activities was to maintain the motivation of his group. This quotation indicates him exercising control to do that:

The engineers themselves were concerned with the future, were frustrated with system inadequacies, and with the fact that the task they were doing did not fully use their skills and knowledge. I therefore began to review the situation with a view to moving some engineers into other groups, and to negotiating with senior management to win other jobs for the group.

He reflected that a number of lessons had been learned from this phase of the change:

Effective leadership does not depend on technical expertise, but on the ability to seek out the vital information, and to use that effectively.

The ability to listen to all levels uncovers a vast amount of untapped and useful information.

Directional changes have been easier to sell under the new style. It is inevitable with changes of this magnitude that complete changes of direction may be forced on the management due to environmental circumstances and competition. It has been easier to get commitment to these changes due to the effective leadership style.

There is a sense here that much of the control of these projects was being carried in the mind of the project managers. They needed to be intuitively scanning the scene, surveying actual or potentially critical issues. Many of the issues were new ones which could not have been anticipated by a formal system. The great ambiguity of many projects meant that relevant data needs could not be fully anticipated. Effective control implied creating a climate in which the team was alert to environmental signals.

Responsiveness alone was not enough. The project manager also needed to be conscious of a lack of communications from the outside world, or from those affected by the project. This could indicate satisfaction and acceptance – but equally it could have been a sign of trouble.

The project manager needs to be active in exercising control – active in stimulating a response from the system at an early stage, to flush out difficulties, while there is still plenty of time for corrective action to be taken. Making a firm proposal stimulates a reaction indicating whether or not a change in direction is needed.

The management of the control agenda in novel and uncertain projects is clearly different from the traditional project control tasks. These have an essential part to play in large projects of this kind. The key lesson is that project managers are using a wider range of methods of control, which emphasize the use of interpersonal skills. These are needed to gather soft information in volatile situations, and to shape, rather than to direct, the flow of events.

Personal checkpoints

- Check how much of the information you have used (rather than received) in the project has come from the formal information system.
- List key events in the project so far, indicating whether or not the formal system helped you to anticipate or deal with them.
- Consider whether or not your experience agrees with the evidence here, that project management depends increasingly on generating internal self-control.
- List informal devices that you have used to help you keep in touch with what is happening on the project.

11

The phases and structures of change

Where are we?

Although often hard to pin-point, change projects have a beginning, a middle and an end. Distinct activities go on at different phases even though the phases themselves overlap and combine. A manager with a clear overview of this sequence will have a better understanding what is going on, and where he or she is getting to.

The balance of driving and restraining forces is likely to alter with each stage, as is the attitude of key stakeholders. While the core interpersonal skills which the project manager has to exercise will be broadly the same at each stage, their focus will change. Knowing where you are is especially useful in projects where progress is likely to be interrupted, and where decisions and plans already made have to be revised.

The phases also provide a structure for the three agendas of change – content, control and process – which we describe in previous chapters. The themes of this chapter are:

Project phases.

Interrupted progress and recycled projects.

Links to the management structure.

Project phases

In relatively unstructured projects, people need more than ever to know where they are, and what is likely to happen next. If they do not, critical phases may be ignored, and energy wasted by tackling an issue at the wrong time.

The audio-diarists clearly concentrated on different issues at successive stages of the change, and handled them in different ways. We have therefore distinguished five broad phases in the change process, as shown in Fig. 11.1. The phases

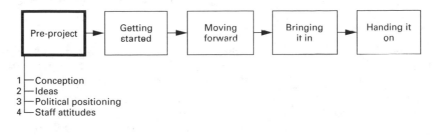

Figure 11.1 The pre-project phase

naturally overlap, but reviewing them separately highlights how the passage of time and events affects the task of project managers.

Pre-project

Past events affect how the job is shaped, and how people view the launch of the latest new idea (Fig. 11.1). There is a time when the project is latent, not yet visible, perhaps not even thought about. Perceptions are being formed about current performance against expected standards, about impending threats or opportunities, and perhaps about ways of dealing with them. During this period the project is conceived – but not yet born. It is not yet clear what its shape or nature will be.

Ideas are tried out, kites are flown, questions asked, informal proposals made and rejected; all far in advance of any formal proposal being made to budget a project, or to give it visibility and public recognition. Things done at this stage nevertheless affect people's attitude and commitment to the change. One diarist recalled a meeting at which he shared his early ideas:

> I volunteered to pull together a group of people from across our other facilities, and put our thoughts together ... we had two five-day meetings and came up with the bare bones of a scheme, which I then drafted into a formal document.

Political moves are made, as key managers seek to protect or enhance their position. If the project is to happen, they will want it set up in a way that has either no effect on their interests, or one that is positive:

> From the UK point of view, the proposal to adopt the same system as the American parent company was a low-risk one, since it was obviously hoped by some of those involved that if anything should go wrong, then the blame

could be placed squarely on the shoulders of those who had made the decision in the USA.

What happens at this stage will affect the job of the project manager, and how it is seen by key players. Their reaction to the project manager will reflect how they fared during this early lobbying, idea-sharing and project-conception stage.

The past affects the attitude and behaviour of other parties as well. Staff who have learned to cope with regular, well-managed change, and who expect that to be part of the job, will generally start with a positive attitude. Those who have been let down by previous changes, or who feel the changes have not been honestly handled, will be distrustful of new proposals, until convinced otherwise. More immediately, the way information about the pre-project phases is communicated to those not yet directly involved will affect their attitude. They will know that something is happening – and whether they are being given the chance to contribute.

Getting started

In this stage the project becomes more visible, and commitments are made, at least to further analysis (Fig. 11.2). If a critical mass of opinion comes together at the

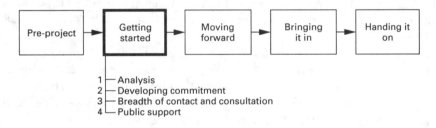

Figure 11.2 Getting started

pre-project stage, the point will be reached at which patterns of past behaviour begin to break, and when those behind the change start work in earnest. Fuller analysis of the (alleged) problem or opportunity is undertaken, the broad feasibility of the proposal assessed, other considerations brought into the picture:

> So having got a statement of business requirements, I was included and asked to take responsibility for developing this maintenance system on behalf of the department ... to have a look at the data, have a look at what the system does, and to see how best to take on board existing data.

> The team has managed to engage the interest of a European staff who represent our European interests, and this is a major step forward.

Decisions emerging in this early phase will shape the later ones. People are investing time and energy in the task, becoming associated with the change, perhaps becoming committed to a particular line. They will rapidly be learning more about the topic (while everyone else is concentrating on their regular job), and will thus be able to shape information and presentations more confidently.

It is thus worth reflecting on how this process is carried out, in this notepad.

Notepad

- *How widely was the study to assess needs or problems drawn in your project?*
- *How many options were compared?*
- *Were the proposals put to management comprehensive and objective, or were they tilted in some way?*
- *Were potential difficulties ignored?*

Whatever is done at this stage, the project manager will have to work with the consequences. If senior management have approved a project that was presented in a way that played up the benefits, while underestimating the costs, then the project manager will have to balance the account at a later stage.

Public commitments are also made at this stage, making later change increasingly difficult, however strong the danger signals. Change projects acquire their own momentum, people's reputations become attached to them, and become difficult to stop. The process of involving others becomes more formal. Project teams and steering groups are established, membership and representation agreed. Is this consultation process covering the right people? Which interest groups are involved, and do they realize the significance of what is being done? Is enough weight given to those expressing reservations or highlighting difficulties, or are they dismissed as 'negative'?

Work can also be done to create an expectation that the change will take place. If people are committed to existing practices, successful change depends on them developing a positive attitude to the project. How this early public, even though still exploratory, phase is handled will shape those attitudes – either preparing the ground for acceptance, or encouraging defensive positions.

Moving forward

This is the time of peak activity on the project, as the detailed work on planning and early implementation takes place (Fig. 11.3). The issue is examined in depth, ideas are generated, searches are undertaken for ready-made solutions, designs are made for unique ones, solutions or approaches are selected, perhaps with pilot installations, and the task of full implementation is planned. Problems and conflicts appear, and work done to solve them. This phase is when the detail needs to be worked on, the implications and pitfalls identified. The problem is, in effect,

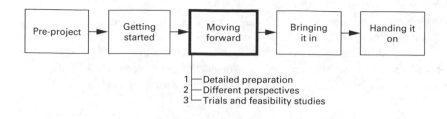

Figure 11.3 Moving forward

opened up to thorough scrutiny and study, looked at from many angles, and then progressively closed down as decisions are made, and plans drawn up. It is ideally a time of exploring and experimenting.

> In planning the refining plant, a small R and D team had been established, and a pilot plant designed and constructed. This was used for producing basic data. It became apparent that the core plant would need to have a pre-treatment stage added, to deal with some corrosive contaminants.

> Things are moving fairly quickly with the artificial intelligence module. We have had some fairly hard but productive sessions around creating the business rules required to input to the model, and the guys who are driving this are coming up with some pretty devastating results.

> I did a cost-benefit analysis of the seven options, which proved particularly hard to do, mainly due to the difficulties of quantifying the financial benefits. Three of the seven gave a positive discounted cash flow, and of those, one, in my eyes anyway, came out as the best.

Different perspectives are brought to bear on the project, a wider constituency given the chance to make a contribution. How many people are being given the chance to take part, and how fully are all those likely to be affected being kept up to date with what is going on? If this is done too narrowly, the manager runs the risk of ignoring key stakeholders, who can cause trouble later. Rumours spread rapidly, and the project staff can quickly find themselves on the defensive if what they are doing starts to be challenged, not necessarily because people object directly to what they are proposing, but because they feel they are being bypassed. The opposite risk is that if too many perspectives are taken into account, too many interests accommodated, then the project will lose focus and direction.

The quality of the work done here will reflect how much commitment and interest has been generated earlier. If people have become convinced that change is necessary, and that the general direction proposed makes sense, their attitude will usually be positive, and they will be willing to give their ideas and enthusiasm to the project. Conversely, problems of commitment during the middle phases of a project often reflect management mistakes in the earlier phases.

Pilot projects

Pilot projects often make sense, providing a good learning device if properly chosen. They can provide valuable information on how an idea might work in practice. Take care to avoid these pitfalls:

- Unclear criteria for evaluating the pilot.
- Pilot site untypical of other operations.
- Staff at pilot site have untypical attitude.
- The move to full operation may be accompanied by other changes, invalidating the predictions from the pilot.
- People become politically committed to the scheme, and unwilling to stop the pilot, once it has become public.
- Pilot 'drifts' into full operation, with no clear review and cut-off points.

Bringing it in

This is the main implementation phase, when visible changes happen, things start to be done in a different way, or in a different place (Fig. 11.4). The separate parts of the change begin to come together, and work becomes more closed in nature, as

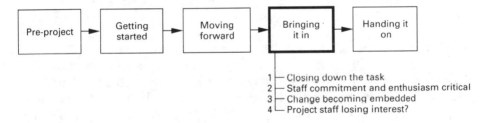

1 ├─ Closing down the task
2 ├─ Staff commitment and enthusiasm critical
3 ├─ Change becoming embedded
4 └─ Project staff losing interest?

Figure 11.4 Bringing it in

what has been agreed and decided is put into effect. The quality of the planning is put to the test. As the plans come up against operating reality, things that were forgotten come to light, as do those that have changed since the plans were made:

An adequate process for the by-products did not avail itself to the project team in time for the refinery completion, and this subsequently had to be cobbled together from some redundant equipment after the refinery was up and running. This was unsatisfactory, but had to be accepted as there had not been sufficient time to develop all the required technology.

Results will also be affected by whether staff have become committed to the project during the earlier stages. If this is the case, then the chances are that implementation will be much easier than if they are indifferent to it, or keen for it to fail. Snags and difficulties inevitably occur. Committed staff will work hard and imaginatively to overcome them, to drive the thing forward, to get satisfaction from solving the problems. They will have a sense of ownership, and will want to make 'their' system work:

> These were difficult days for everyone concerned, since it involved working almost continuously at the plant for a six-month period. These days were long and demanding, and even some of the younger men found it difficult to maintain attention and enthusiasm. However, such attention and dedication was sustained that the process began to generate good quality products at good rates.

Some projects also face the difficulty at this phase that the normal work often still needs to be done during a change-over, which imposes extra pressures on staff.

A critical feature of this phase is the extent to which the change becomes thoroughly embedded. Organizational changes have to compete with the forces of inertia and habit, as well as those of opposition. Forms and appearances may change, while underneath people revert to established ways of operating. Project managers need to ensure that consolidation occurs, that people learn how to use the new methods successfully, that they become confident in the new styles or ways of working.

Difficulties which might encourage reversion need to be convincingly overcome, and people able to experience tangible, valued benefits. The changes need to be reinforced, by publicizing successes and benefits, and by regular action to maintain the new ways. If signs of falling back appear, the reasons need to be examined urgently, and action taken to make that approach less attractive.

As this phase itself draws to a close, project management face the problem of the commitment of their own staff working on the change. People are attracted to this kind of work by the novelty and excitement of a new challenge, the unfamiliar problem, the clear field on which to play. As the task concludes, vital details still need to be dealt with, loose ends tied up, or the change will be in danger of unravelling. Tying up these loose ends is often difficult and unglamorous work – and staff will be thinking of their next career move.

Handing it on

In this phase, the change becomes normality, members of the project team disperse to other activities, the benefits of the change begin to show (Fig. 11.5). It is important here to ensure that a proper handover has taken place between project

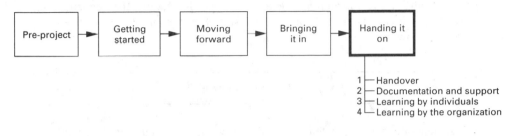

Figure 11.5 Handing it on

staff working on the change and the line staff who will have to live with it thereafter. The project work has to become bonded into the organization. Work that has been done by the project team, and has perhaps been taken for granted, may need to be taken on by regular staff. Users of a new computer system have probably got into the habit of asking project staff for help with problems – whom do they go to when the project staff have gone, or are working on another project?

Information has been built up during the project which is vital to the running of the system – has it been documented and passed on? Skills have been developed and used by those closest to the change – have they become widespread in the organization, or is the change vulnerable to the loss of a few key staff?

Successful change will often set off a learning process for individuals. Unexpected benefits can be realized as people become familiar with a new approach, and more confident at using it. Deliberate actions can be taken to ensure that people not only learn to use new methods successfully, but start to apply their enhanced abilities in unforeseen ways. What is being done to enable the organization as a whole to learn from the project? Post-implementation audits are a way of reviewing how a project was handled to see what can be learned by those concerned, to enable them to learn from the experience. They are not often conducted.

Notepad

- *Which of these phases has your own project reached?*
- *Have the demands on you and the project team changed as each phase has been undertaken? How have these changes in demands been coped with?*
- *How have events at one stage affected events at later ones, for better or worse?*

Interrupted progress and recycled projects

While it is simple, and useful, to set out the phases of a project as we have done above, projects never move through that sequence in an orderly way. They are in practice subject to interruptions, delays and speed-ups, and the recycling and replanning which has to be done as a result. Some examples from the diary projects follow.

Policy changes

- A new option is suggested, which delays work on the current plan, while the new approach is evaluated.
- The budget for the project is cancelled or cut, perhaps for reasons unconnected with the project itself.
- A new project evaluation rule or procedure is introduced, against which the project has to be reassessed.
- A change in wider company policy requires the project to be implemented much earlier than was originally intended.
- Other people hear about a promising result from the project, and encourage the project team to complete it more quickly, so as to take advantage of the innovation.
- One business unit changes its policy about how it is going to schedule orders, resulting in a reconsideration of their part in a wider order-scheduling programme.

Organizational factors

- A department that is required to make a decision before the project moves forward, delays the decision.
- A department experiences severe problems in its core business, and cannot devote the time required to a new project.
- Delay while additional financial support, recently found to be necessary, is achieved.
- Criticism or opposition from users or other affected parties leads to a review and replanning of the change.
- Implementation delayed when it is realized that people's knowledge and skill are not yet up to the standards required.
- User needs found to have been incorrectly specified.

Technical factors

- Action cannot proceed until the results of analyses and investigations are received.

- Significant problems occur with a new and complex process, requiring considerable redesign work to be done.
- Equipment or procedures are found not to work, requiring a delay for repair, and perhaps a recycle to an earlier phase to make a different approach possible.
- System not reflecting user requirements.
- The basic technology for part of the project had not been completed by the time the rest was ready to go in.
- A subcontractor does not complete work to a satisfactory standard, and has to be replaced.
- Construction is delayed by the wettest summer in over a century.

These delays, interruptions and revisions to plan were sources of great difficulty to many of the audio-diarists. They appear, nevertheless, to be a common characteristic of large change projects, especially those with changing goals and wide linkages.

The process can be expressed as in Fig. 11.6 of the project phases, to which interruptions from inside and outside the project have been added.

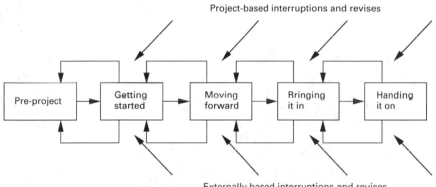

Figure 11.6 Sources of project interruptions

To one manager, expecting a reasonably structured passage through the project task:

all these interruptions appeared as burning arrows that tried to block the structured and goal-directed progress of the project.

But on reflection he concluded that:

looking at the process more objectively, it must be realized that these interrupts are quite normal in strategic projects. The way we handled these interrupts improved the quality of the decision-making.

This last comment is worth emphasizing. Given the volatility of the environment in which most change projects take place, and given the novelty and uncertainty of many of the changes themselves, it is to be expected that there will be false starts.

New information generated during the project may show that things are going in the wrong direction. Ignoring that unwelcome news is likely to be much more damaging to the project than the delays incurred while plans are reviewed and revised in the light of new knowledge – difficult and frustrating though that will undoubtedly be for the project manager.

Notepad

- *Can you list the changes to plan, interruptions, delays, etc., that have occurred on your project?*
- *On reflection, were the resulting changes beneficial to the final outcome?*
- *Should there have been more reviews and revisions to plan, rather than fewer, as new information became available?*

This variable, interrupted nature of progress emphasizes again the need for a greater value to be placed on the influencing skills of the project manager. Few, if any, of the interruptions illustrated above were predictable – and could not have been included in a structured project plan in anything more than the most general way.

When interruptions hit the project, they cause disruption and aggravation to those concerned; but at the same time require a constructive and positive response. It falls to the project manager to use what influence he or she has to persuade others to retain their commitment, to revise what they were doing, to change direction – in the full knowledge that further changes may be just around the corner. That calls for influencing and interpersonal skills of a high order.

Links to the management structure

If a project is to succeed, it needs at some point to be linked to the management structure. However innovative and entrepreneurial the proposal, it will at some point require resources. A clear link to the management structure also helps to ensure that it remains aligned to business developments, and is kept consistent with other changes.

The project champion, or the project manager, needs to work on three issues:

1. **Structural links.** How is the project team linked to the wider structure? Does the project manager report directly to a senior manager, to a special sub-committee of the Board, or what? Is this arrangement still appropriate, as other events change duties and responsibilities?
2. **Reporting links.** How is information passed to and from the project team? Is

there a regular spot on the Board agenda at which the project is discussed, or is it done in an *ad hoc* way? What needs to be done to ensure that relevant information from senior management reaches the project in time to use it?

3. **Managing the sponsor.** What information or other support does the sponsor need to help them to represent the needs of the project to higher management? What communication channels already exist, and are they adequate? If not, what other routes can be created?

Notepad

*   *How is your project linked to the rest of the organization?*
*   *Is top management adequately informed about what is going on?*
*   *Is the project kept up to date in any formal way with relevant developments elsewhere in the business, or does it depend on the grapevine?*

Personal checkpoints

---

*   Identify where your project has got to in the sequence of phases set out above.
*   What do the notes above suggest as the critical things you should be concentrating on?
*   Review how interruptions and delays were handled, to see if constructive use was made of the hold-up.
*   Review how the project ties in to the management structure. Have those links been properly maintained, kept in good working order?

12

Take the lead

How different is the task?

The studies reported in this book have shown both what is different and what is similar about the task of managing change projects. These were summed up in the first chapter and are repeated in Table 12.1. This suggests that managing 'normal' operations would involve the manager in dealing with a relatively predictable task, done by staff who know each other both as people and in terms of their roles and working relationships. The basis of the manager's authority is relatively clear, and well-established methods of coordination are available, using established sources and channels of information. Momentum to get the task done will be maintained by pressure from those in other roles around the organization, whose own performance in part depends on it.

Table 12.1 Managing systems and projects

	System	*Project*
Task	Familiar	Unfamiliar
Staff	Designated, known	Diverse, temporary
Roles and duties	Established patterns	Uncertain, variable
Culture	Role or power	Task
Working relationships	Established cooperation	Negotiable
Authority	Clear, reflects position	Ambiguous, little direct
Coordination	Hierarchical	Network/matrix
Information sources	Established, routine	New, uncertain
Learning and attitude change	Desirable	Essential
Momentum	Maintained by system	Threatened by system
Time horizon	Extended, long-term	Bounded, finite

Managing a change project is different. The task will often be unfamiliar, done by staff who are working together as a temporary team, with longer-term responsibilities elsewhere in the organization. The manager's direct authority over the project team, and over those whose support is needed, will typically be ambiguous, with coordination of an uncertain task depending on equally uncertain sources of information. Momentum can easily be lost, as the priorities of other managers in the organization are likely to emphasize delivering on current operations, from which the change project threatens to distract them.

What are the basic steps?

Faced with handling a change project, however ambiguous, the core task of the project manager is to reduce the uncertainty of the situation, so that confident action can be taken to move events in the desired direction.

Steps that will help reduce that uncertainty which we have highlighted through the book are as follows:

Identify and manage stakeholders
Establishing who has an interest in the change, who is likely to support or undermine it, assessing what their interests are, and planning how to get their support or deflect their opposition.

Work on objectives
Ensuring that an often vague and ill-defined proposal is turned into something which stakeholders understand, accept and identify with, so that they are able to see what they need to do, and to focus their energy on a common target.

Set a full content agenda
As well as setting objectives, ensuring that the other items on the content agenda are identified and included in the project plan. The novelty of the task implies that issues can easily be omitted, causing failure later. Technical, organizational and people issues are all likely to need some attention, as are the links between them.

Build appropriate control systems
The project manager needs to know what is happening – even when the novelty of the project means it is not clear what should be happening. Formal control systems help, but internal control by those working on the project helps more, as does an ability to gather unplanned, unstructured signals about the state of events and attitudes.

Plan the process of change
How change is introduced is as important to acceptance and commitment as the nature of the change itself. In the pressure for results in a fast-moving situation, adequate attention to the process aspects will speed up a project, not delay it. Key issues to deal with under the process agenda are listed below.

Establishing roles

Since those who have to work on the project will not have done so before, it needs to be clearly worked out with them, and those they work for, what the project expects of them, and what they can expect in return.

Build a project team

A major tool of project management, project teams cannot be taken for granted. Conscious management of the team, including, if possible, adjusting the membership in the light of the skills present and needed, is more likely to produce results than leaving it to chance.

Nurture coalitions of support

Change projects threaten established patterns of work and power within the organization. The manager working to implement such a change is bound to come up against opposition, indifference or apathy, which can quickly sap enthusiasm. Identifying people who will give powerful support to the change is essential to counter looming inertia. So also is the need do things which reduce the resistance of people to the change, and secures their interest and support.

Communicate relentlessly

Arguably the most essential aspect of the whole project management task, this means ensuring that structures for communicating are set up, and used effectively. This allows information about the change, and about changes to the change, to be widely shared. Also that information moves in both directions, passing information around, and feeding the control system.

Recognize power

Lacking formal power, project managers nevertheless need to influence others to do things. They therefore have to be alert to where power lies in the system, how to use it to their advantage, and how to use, build and nurture what power they have.

Handing on

Even if the project comes to an apparently successful conclusion, it is easy for the forces of inertia or opposition to reassert themselves, and undermine or reverse what has been achieved. This implies conscious efforts to embed the change in the organization, and to ensure that the maintenance of the change is a realistic part of someone's role.

Interpersonal skills for project managers

Clearly the effective management of a change project requires the exercise of a range of analytical and planning techniques, especially when the project is large, with many sub-projects having to come together at the right time. These approaches feature strongly in the early education and training programmes of the professions from which many project managers are drawn; and they also make up most of the training available in project management.

The argument of this book has been that a new emphasis is needed. To cope with the introduction of novel changes in a volatile environment, skills other than simply those of analysis and structured methods are needed. The change in emphasis, we believe, suggested by this study is to place more reliance on the acquisition and use of a range of interpersonal skills. These enable the change manager to work more effectively in the uncertain and political environments surrounding major change projects, and to take the lead in managing the different interests involved.

In the earlier chapters, we have outlined these skills, and ways in which they can be used and improved by project managers. None of the interpersonal skills outlined above is new, and none is particularly difficult to improve. The project manager willing to change the emphasis of his or her work, so as to give rather more attention to the interpersonal, process aspects of management, will do a better and more satisfying job.

As in all aspects of management development, small, incremental steps are more likely to succeed. A self-development project to improve their own interpersonal skills, starting now, could be the project manager's most valuable investment.

A guide to further reading

This list includes details of all books referred to in the text, as well as others which the authors believe may interest readers of this book.

Belbin, M. (1981) *Management Teams*, Heinemann, London.
   This explains in detail the idea of team roles, and the ways in which different combinations affect performance.
Dawson, M. (1990) *Opportunities for Change*, The Industrial Society Press, London.
   A wealth of practical advice on specific change implementation techniques, some familiar, some less so.
Gunton, T. (1990) *Inside Information Technology: A practical guide to management issues*, Prentice Hall, Hemel Hempstead.
   A critical perspective on traditional project management and change implementation methods, as applied to management information systems projects.
Handy, C. (1990) *Inside Organizations*, BBC Publications, London.
   Includes ideas and techniques relevant to the management of change.
Kanter, R. M. (1983) *The Change Masters: Corporate entrepreneurs at work*, George Allen & Unwin, London.
Keen, P. (1981) 'Information systems and organizational change', in E. Rhodes and D. Wield (eds), *Implementing New Technologies: Choice, decision and change in manufacturing*, Basil Blackwell/The Open University, Oxford.
   An article which fascinatingly describes the tactics of counter-implementation, with suggestions on how to against them. The book in which it is reprinted contains other articles on change management.
Mayon-White, B. (ed.) (1986) *Planning and Managing Change*, Open University, Milton Keynes.
Pettigrew, A.M. (ed.) (1988) *The Management of Strategic Change*, Basil Blackwell, Oxford.
Woodcock, M. (1989) *Team Development Manual* (2nd edn), Gower, Aldershot.

Index